PERFECTLY HEDGED

Interested in learning more?
In-person and online training available.
Visit our website for additional information.

Join the Perfectly Hedged community!
Follow us on LinkedIn for new insights, updates and exclusive offers.

Let's connect, I'd love to hear from you:

SAMUEL BASI
Founder & Author
Perfectly Hedged LLC

+1 203-391-8021
samuel.basi@perfectlyhedged.com
www.perfectlyhedged.com
linkedin.com/company/perfectly-hedged-llc

For rights and permissions, please contact:

Samuel.Basi@perfectlyhedged.com

About The Author

After graduating with a bachelor's degree (with honors) in economics from the University of Loughborough, United Kingdom, Samuel Basi embarked on a successful, and ongoing career in commodity trading.

Samuel started his career at Trafigura, one of the largest commodity trading houses in the world. He has worked the last fifteen years in the commodity industry across multiple commodities, desks, and continents.

Initially in Switzerland, then in the US, Samuel spent time in operations, on the deals desk, physical trading, and derivative trading. He has developed a broad knowledge base of almost all parts of the commodity trading business.

Gaining exposure to all facets of commodity trading has placed Samuel in the position to write this book in an effort to simplify hedging, a subject that is absolutely key to the long-term sustainability of commodity firms but is often misunderstood, poorly explained, and the cause of sizable losses that could otherwise be avoided.

Because both of his parents were teachers for 40 years, it seemed only fitting that he use this platform to help others understand this key skill so they can further their careers.

Table Of Contents

1. Introduction

Over the course of this book, I am going to simplify and explain hedging, and detail the ways it is used in the base metals industry. This knowledge will be useful for everyone from back to middle office. Middle office jobs can go by many names: traffic, co-ordinator, scheduler, operations, and they can have varying responsibilities, but they are all positions where a good understanding of hedging will dramatically improve the quality of your work. This book may even be worth a refresher for some in the front office!

Although it can seem highly technical, hedging is a relatively simple concept. I don't say that to patronize you if it is a concept you have struggled with in the past. I'm trying to put your mind at ease; when explained well, hedging is not a topic to be nervous about. Having this knowledge should embolden you to be confident in your work and a variety of situations that may arise on a daily basis.

Unfortunately, commodity firms are often sink-or-swim environments. I have seen firsthand many intelligent, talented employees fall behind or, worse, lose their jobs because of issues stemming from not understanding hedging properly. Multiple times I have heard the following question or a variation of it asked by an operator early in their career: "We bought copper at $8,000/metric ton (mt), and now we are selling it at $7,000/mt-how are we still making money? Why aren't we losing $1,000/mt?"

Often, the operator is harshly judged for not knowing the answer. This creates a negative loop in which the operator feels frustrated, is still confused, neglects to ask those pertinent questions going forward, and is more likely to make a mistake related to hedging. When an inevitable mistake occurs, the company loses money, and very often the operator loses their job. Both of these outcomes are entirely avoidable. Throughout the course of this book, you will learn the answer to the above question along with a solid base of knowledge that will serve you throughout your career.

This book is not going to lay out a trading strategy, but will go step-by-step into what hedging is, why it is important, and how it relates to your work. Incidentally, if you've reached for this book in error and you were looking for a Holy Grail trading strategy, I can save you some time-there isn't one. Anyone telling you otherwise is likely trying to scam you. If, despite this warning, you still believe that there is a get-rich-quick route to trading, I have a bridge in Brooklyn to sell you.

2. What Hedging Is and Why It Is Necessary

At its core, hedging is not a trading strategy; it is a risk mitigation system. It is used by companies up and down the supply chain as a method to reduce or even eliminate exposure to changes in the price of the commodity they are producing, consuming, or trading. It can also be used as a tool to lock in a profit margin where production/consumption costs are known. Whether you work for a miner, a refined metal producer, a metal consumer, or a trading company, hedging is a key part of the industry.

Metal prices are set on **exchanges** around the world and are entirely outside of the control of the companies that trade on them. Hedging allows companies to become **agnostic** to the volatile price fluctuations that can happen to these commodities on a daily basis. That is not to say companies do not care about the price of a commodity, even if they hedge. The price of a commodity also affects financing costs, borrowing utilization rates, and margins owed on derivative positions, among a host of other impacts-just ask your finance department next time there is a 10 percent rally in the price. However, when you hedge material correctly, your profit on that trade will not be impacted by subsequent movements in the outright price of that commodity.

Most of the time, hedging a commodity involves entering into a **futures contract** on a relevant exchange. A futures contract is when you agree to buy or sell a specified tonnage of a commodity at an agreed price at a specific date in the future.

I will explain in greater detail in Chapter 4 the mechanics of exactly how a futures hedge is executed and why that mitigates price risk, but for now the important takeaway is this: a hedge is an **equal and opposite** futures position to the physical metal transaction.

If you are physically buying a commodity, 1,000 mt of aluminum for example, and you are agreeing on a price of $2,500/mt. Hedging that purchase would mean that at the same time as buying your physical material, you sell 1,000 mt of aluminum futures at the same price of

$2,500/mt. If, in this example, you were selling 1,000 mt of physical aluminum at $2,500/mt, your hedge would be to buy 1,000 mt of aluminum futures at $2,500/mt.

Not every commodity can be hedged in this way. In order to hedge accurately, the commodity you transact in needs to have a tradable futures contract on an exchange you can access and that is liquid enough for the volume you physically buy or sell. The price of the commodity you trade in also needs to be highly correlated to the price set by the exchange. There are plenty of commodities where price is set exclusively by the companies that trade it or by a publication, not on an exchange. In these instances, hedging using futures contracts is not possible, and the companies that trade them will either try to fix the price of their purchases and sales at the same time (often referred to as a back-to-back business), or they will hope the price goes up when they buy (going long) or vice versa when they sell (going short).

Hedging can take different forms, depending on exactly what business your company operates in. Even if a company trades a commodity that does have a liquid futures exchange, they may not utilize futures. If a company has a purchase and a sale of the same commodity transacting at the same time and price, they essentially have a natural hedge. For example, a producer pricing their input material at the same time on the same market as their output material, may already be mitigating their price exposure.

Chapter Summary

- Hedging is a tool commodity companies can use to mitigate price risk that is outside their control. It allows them to become price-agnostic.
- Hedging can take different forms, but the most common utilizes futures contracts.
- A hedge is an equal and opposite futures position to the physical metal transaction.
- Not all commodities can be hedged using futures.

3. How Metal Prices Are Determined

In this chapter, I will give a brief explanation of the two most commonly used exchanges for metals trading outside of China: the **London Metal Exchange (LME)** and the **Chicago Mercantile Exchange (CME)**. These are the two exchanges you will almost certainly be exposed to. I will also explain the price setting mechanisms for each exchange, because there are some key differences between the two.

Knowing every detail about an exchange and how it functions may not be necessary for your day-to-day job. However, I have found that having some basic knowledge about the exchanges commodity companies trade on enhances employees' understanding of why and how metals trade the way they do, and why hedging is so important to the long-term profitability of commodity companies.

LME

The LME is the oldest metal trading exchange in the world. Initially founded in 1877 (but with roots going back as far as the opening of the Royal Exchange in London in 1571), it is the largest metal exchange in the world, used by traders across the globe as the main source for price discovery for base metals. Currently, the LME trades aluminum, aluminum alloy, cobalt, copper, lead, nasaac, nickel, steel, tin, and zinc. Some of these metals are much more liquid than others, meaning the volume of futures contracts traded daily are much higher than others. It is going to be easier to hedge large tonnage of metal on markets with higher liquidity (aluminum, copper, lead, zinc, nickel) compared to the lower liquidity markets (aluminum alloy, cobalt, nasaac, steel, tin).

The LME is unique in a couple of ways compared to other exchanges. Although most trading volume is now executed through the LME's online trading platform, the official prices from the second trading session each day are still set using open outcry. Traders will shout prices to each other, use hand signals, and relay those prices back to clerks who have clients on multiple phones, buying and selling all in real time.

The area where traders shout prices across to each other is known as the **ring**. While today the ring comprises red leather sofas set in a circle, it originally got its name when metals trading moved to the Jerusalem Coffee House in the early 19th century. When all the traders had gathered, a circle would be drawn in chalk on the floor, and they would stand around the ring to trade. While the ring and its long-term viability are a constant discussion, for now, floor traders still make their way to the ring two times per day, where a five-minute trading session for each metal is used to set official prices. The last official session of the day is called the **kerb** and is now carried out electronically with closing prices being determined using a volume weighted average pricing mechanism (VWAP). The kerb gets its name from the same era as the chalk ring. In the early days of the LME, traders who wanted to continue trading after time was up would step outside onto the street and trade on the kerb of the pavement (curb of the sidewalk).

To trade directly on the LME requires an LME membership-these memberships range from category 1 (the highest) to category 7 (the lowest). The privileges of membership decrease as the membership category lowers. Only category 1 through 4 members can trade directly on the LME. This does not mean that everyone who hedges their physical metal has to be an LME member, but it does mean they will utilize LME brokers who are LME members.

Access to the LME ring is reserved for brokers with a Category 1 membership. As of the time of writing, eight companies are Category 1 LME members. Only traders from these companies are allowed to sit in the ring and take part in the **open outcry** sessions. In each five-minute trading session, official prices are set for **cash** and **three-month (3M)** prompts, which are the last prices bid and offered for each prompt date for each metal. The online platform of the LME is open for trade from 1 a.m. London until 7 p.m. London every business day.

The other unique aspect of the LME is that (barring steel and cash settled futures contracts) LME trades have settlement dates every business day of the year (on a rolling three-month basis), where most other exchanges have only one settlement date per month. The date a trade settles is known as the **prompt date**. If you wish, you can obtain a price for a settlement date, from as nearby as "**tom**" trades that settle the following business day, cash trades that settle in two business days (such as the **official cash** settlement trades), to as far out as five to ten years in the case of some metals. Typically, the further out a settlement date is needed, the less liquidity there will be, which will affect the value of that trade.

Base metal prices are obtained by LME brokers through the trading of **lots**. One lot of metal is defined by the LME as an exact number of metric tons for each metal as follows:

- Aluminum/copper/lead/zinc: 25 mt
- Aluminum alloy/nasaac: 20 mt
- Steel: 10 mt
- Nickel: 6 mt
- Tin: 5 mt
- Cobalt: 1 mt

You can only trade in whole lot sizes, so if you buy 2 lots of LME copper, you will be buying 50 mt of copper. You may have heard someone asking to buy or sell a number, then the metal. For example, "Where can I buy 10 December Ali?" means they want to buy 10 lots of December aluminum, equaling 250 mt. When hedging material, the brokers you may be dealing with (either internal or external) will generally talk in terms of number of lots rather than outright tonnage of metal. I suggest you become familiar with your multiplication tables, particularly twenty-five!

Outside of the official prices set in each of the three rings and the kerb, you are probably somewhat familiar with the prices you have seen flashing on screens. This price is known as the three-month price. If someone asks what the price of aluminum is, they are more than likely referencing the screen price, which is the 3M price. The reason the prices quoted on the screen are a three-month prompt date is because that was the approximate length of a voyage for a vessel carrying copper from Chile to the UK and tin from Malaysia to the UK at the time the exchange was founded.

Part of the reason I was initially drawn to commodity trading is because it is impossible to escape how interconnected your trading activity is to the real world. Traders needed a price for their copper and tin that reflected the reality of an actual vessel's arrival to its destination. Your activities have a real world impact by forming a vital part of the supply chain for so many everyday products, and details like the LME 3M price are part of what keep me engaged and excited to be part of this industry.

CME

The CME was established in 1848 as the world's first futures exchange. However, it was not until 2008 when the CME group acquired the NYMEX group-including their commodities exchange division (COMEX)-that base metal trading was brought under the CME umbrella. As of the time of this writing, copper is the only base metal that trades on the CME exchange with high volume compared to the LME. The vast majority of domestic copper producers and consumers in the US use CME prices for their physical contracts instead of the LME. Recently, the CME aluminum futures contract has seen an increase in volume, so we may over time see a real competitor to LME aluminum develop. The CME does have futures contracts for both lead and zinc, but at the time of writing, the open interest (total number of outstanding contracts) for these metals is extremely low. The CME has launched a cobalt contract which with the rise in electric vehicles globally, is starting to pick up volume. They are also the main liquidity provider for US and EU hot rolled coil (HRC) steel, and their lithium hydroxide contract has also seen huge growth over the last two years. The CME are (at the time of writing) making a real push on their molybdenum oxide contract - other exchanges have attempted this in the past without much luck, here is hoping the CME succeed in their attempt.

Base metals trading on the CME is entirely electronic and trades 23 hours a day, 5 days a week. For all metals trading hours are 6 P.M. Eastern time US until 5 P.M. Easten time US the following day, Sunday - Friday.

Unlike the LME, a futures contract on the CME only has one prompt date per month-the last business day of that month. For copper, the CME also has what are called active months: March, May, July, September, and December. These five months are by far the most traded prompts for CME copper. You can trade any forward month up to 24 months out, but the liquidity is extremely low on the non-active months.

Just like on the LME, CME copper is traded in lots, but where the LME trades in metric tons, CME copper trades in pounds (lbs), with one copper lot representing 25,000 lbs. This roughly equals 11.34 mt. The prices for CME copper are quoted in dollars and cents per pound. Trades are in whole lots, so you can only trade in multiples of 25,000 lbs. This means if you buy four lots of CME copper, you will be buying 100,000 lbs. CME aluminum, lead, and zinc trade in metric tons, and the lot size is 25 mt. Prices are quoted in dollars per metric ton, the same as on the LME. CME cobalt trades in dollars and cents per pound, and each lot is 2204.62 lbs, which equals exactly one mt. US HRC trades in lots of 20 short tons (1 short ton is equal to 2,000 lbs) and is quoted in dollars per short ton. Lithium hydroxide trades in 1,000 kg lots and is quoted in dollars per kg. Molybdenum oxide trades in 1,322.77 lb lots and is quoted in dollars and cents per pound. EU HRC lot sizes are 20 mt and it is quoted in euros per metric ton.

Similar to LME trading, you will still need to place your orders through a broker registered on the CME to trade CME futures.

While the CME does not have open outcry trading for base metals, it does still have a settlement price each day, known as the **trade at settlement (TAS)** price. However, some of your customers may also refer to it as the market on close (MOC) price. Although the market trades twenty-three hours a day, this settlement price is generated at 1 p.m. ET/12 p.m. CT.

Prices on both the LME and CME are quoted using a **bid** and **offer** (offer is also referred to as **ask**) system. If you are looking at the prices on the screen, the bid is the price you could currently sell at and the offer, or ask, is the price you could currently buy at. If you need a quick reminder, the bid, where you can sell, is always going to be the lower of the two prices, and the offer is the higher of the two. This is pretty logical-if you could sell at a higher price than you could buy, you would be printing money!

It is important to note a specific number of lots will be bid or offered for each price. This means there is a finite number of lots you could buy or sell at any given price. For example, if there are five lots of LME 3M copper bid at $8,500/mt, this means the most you could sell at that price at that given time would be five lots. If you wanted to sell ten lots of LME 3M copper at that current market, you would receive five lots at $8,500/MT and then five lots at the next best bid, provided there was enough volume. This is known as **order depth**.

When looking at the 3M price on LME or a forward month price on the CME or LME, it is worth clarifying that this is not a prediction of where prices will be in three months. These are simply the prices that based on the conditions in the market at that time, someone agreed to buy or sell that metal for settlement at a date in the future. The price quoted on the screen is rarely valid for more than a few seconds at a time, let alone days or months.

A common feature between the LME and the CME is that they are both **physically settled** exchanges. A caveat to this are steel contracts on the LME and cobalt contracts on the CME, which are **cash settled**. Physically settled means that every lot traded on each exchange is linked to a physical parcel of metal that sits in an exchange-approved warehouse, somewhere around the world. These physical parcels are called **warrants**. If a futures position is held to expiry, it will become an obligation to either take delivery from or deliver metal into one of these warehouses. Chapter 10 will detail warrants in much greater detail.

One final key difference between the exchanges is that an LME future only becomes a physical obligation on its prompt date. A futures contract on the CME can become a physical obligation on any day from the start of the prompt month, depending on if your particular futures position is called on for delivery.

Chapter Summary

- Below you will find a quick comparison between the LME and the CME:

	LME	CME
Metals Traded	Aluminum, Aluminum Alloy, Cobalt, Copper, Lead, Nasaac, Nickel, Steel, Tin, Zinc	Aluminum, Cobalt, Copper, Lead, Lithium Hydroxide, Molybdenum Oxide, Steel, Zinc
Prompt Dates Available	Every business day on a rolling 3-month basis	The last business day of each month
Trading Method	Open Outcry, Electronic	Electronic
Trading Hours	1 a.m. London until 7 p.m. London, Monday - Friday.	Copper, Zinc: 6 p.m. ET until 5 p.m. ET the following day, Sunday-Friday Aluminum, Cobalt, Lead: 5 p.m. ET until 4 p.m. ET the following day, Sunday-Friday
Lot Sizes	Aluminum, Copper, Lead, Zinc: 25 mt Aluminum Alloy, Nasaac: 20 mt Steel: 10 mt Nickel: 6 mt Tin: 5 mt Cobalt: 1 mt	Copper: 25,000 lbs Aluminum, Lead, Zinc: 25 mt Cobalt: 2204.62 lbs North European HRC Steel: 20 mt U.S. Midwest HRC Steel: 20 Short tons Lithium Hydroxide: 1,000 kg Molybdenum Oxide: 1,322.77lbs
Price Quotation	USD/mt	Copper, Cobalt: USD/lbs Aluminum, Lead, Zinc: USD/mt U.S. Midwest HRC Steel: USD/Short ton Lithium Hydroxide: USD/Kg North European HRC Steel: €/mt

- The LME and the CME are the two primary exchanges for base metals futures trading outside of China.
- Orders are placed through brokers who hold membership on the LME and CME and facilitate price discovery.
- Prices are quoted on both exchanges using a bid and offer system.
- 3M prices on the LME, or forward prices on the CME are not a prediction of where prices will be at that settlement time.
- Both exchanges, with the exception of steel on the LME and cobalt on the CME, are physically settled exchanges.

4. Hedging in Practice

Companies cannot afford to take the risk that prices will move in their favor. Hedging is the most prudent mechanism to ensure profit margins will not be impacted by the volatility in metal prices.

There are many ways to fix the price of a physical contract. You may be pricing your physical, live using screen prices. You could be using a single-day settlement price or the average of multiple days settlements. You might be fixing the price over a full monthly average. Regardless of what mechanism you are using to fix the price of your physical contract, to hedge that contract you will be taking action over the same time period on the futures market.

As mentioned in Chapter 2, in order to hedge physical metal, you will enter into a futures contract that is equal in price and tonnage and opposite in direction to the physical deal you are hedging. For example, if you are buying 100 mt of copper at $8,000/mt, you will at the same time sell 100 mt of copper futures at $8,000/mt. Let's say you sell those same 100 mt of copper three weeks later and the price of copper is now $7,500/mt, you would also buy 100 mt of copper futures at $7,500/mt. As shown in Table 1, you have mitigated the risk of the copper price falling between physical purchase and sale.

Table 1

	mt	$/mt	Cash Flow
Physical Purchase	100	$8,000	$(800,000)
Futures Sale	-100	$8,000	$800,000
Physical Sale	-100	$7,500	$750,000
Futures Purchase	100	$7,500	$(750,000)
			$ -

If you didn't hedge your purchase and the same scenario occurred, the copper price decreased by $500/mt in between fixing the purchase and the sale, you would have lost $500/mt as shown in Table 2.

Table 2

	mt	$/mt	Cash Flow
Physical Purchase	100	$8,000	$(800,000)
Physical Sale	-100	$7,500	$750,000
			$(50,000)

Conversely, hedging does mean that if the price of copper were to increase from $8,000/mt to $8,500/mt from the time of your purchase to your sale, you do not receive that $500/mt gain from the increase in price. But the point here is that you have no idea whether the copper price is going to move up or down in that time period. Hedging allows you to protect yourself against price movements that are often drastic.

Some types of trading such as concentrates trading or scrap trading utilize payables (the amounts you will pay a supplier for the metal) that are percentages, either of the commodity and/or of the exchange price, based on the chemical analysis of that material. Concentrates hedging is also affected by moisture levels. When a metal concentrate is mined, it will contain a certain amount of moisture. No one is going to pay for water weight-so the payable, and therefore hedgeable tonnage is adjusted for this. The gross tonnage (including moisture) of a concentrates parcel is referred to as the wet metric tonnage (wmt). The tonnage you will calculate your hedging requirements from, adjusted for the moisture level, is referred to as the dry metric tonnage (dmt).

For example, a copper concentrate may only contain 25 percent copper, and the industry standard payable for copper is 96.5 percent of that contained copper. A 10,000 wmt copper concentrate shipment with a moisture level of 8% would equate to a dmt of 9,200 (10,000wmt * 92% non-moisture). Using a copper payable at 96.5 percent and 25 percent copper content would equate to a hedgeable tonnage of 2,225 to the nearest 25mt lot (9,200dmt * 96.5% payable copper * 25% copper contained). Whenever you have a metal contract where the payable is less than 100 percent, you only hedge the metal contained, payable tonnage. In this example, that would be 2,225 mt of copper as shown in table 3.

Table 3

	10,000 wmt (8% moisture, 25% Cu @ 96.5% Payable)	$/mt	Cash Flow
Physical Purchase	2,225	$8,000	$(17,800,000)
Futures Sale	-2,225	$8,000	$17,800,000
Physical Sale	-2,225	$9,000	$20,025,000
Futures Purchase	2,225	$9,000	$(20,025,000)
			$ -

If you were to hedge this contract on the gross wmt instead of the payable, contained copper on the dmt, you would actually be creating price risk instead of mitigating it. As seen in Table 4, this could easily cause large losses. By hedging the full wmt of the concentrates shipment of 10,000 wmt, you have over hedged by 7,775 mt, creating a large exposure. The price has risen $1,000/mt between pricing the purchase and sale. You are only able to charge 96.5% of 25 percent of the 9,200 dmt on the sale so while you gain $1,000/mt on the 2,225 mt of payable physical, you have lost $1,000/mt on 10,000 mt of futures, creating a hedge loss of $7,775,000 as shown in table 4.

Table 4

	10,000 wmt (8% moisture, 25% Cu @ 96.5% Payable)	$/mt	Cash Flow
Physical Purchase	2,225	$8,000	$(17,800,000)
Futures Sale	-10,000	$8,000	$80,000,000
Physical Sale	-2,225	$9,000	$20,025,000
Futures Purchase	10,000	$9,000	$(90,000,000)
			$(7,775,000)

You might be asking, if we are selling futures at the same price as we are buying physical, and we buy futures at the same price as we are selling physical, how are we making money? While answers vary between products and there are many additional ways to extract profits, the main answer to that question is below for refined metal, concentrates, and scrap.

<u>Refined Metal/Value-Added Products</u>

Refined metal and value-added products trade at **premiums** to exchange set prices. This premium is indicative of (and this is not an exhaustive list), production costs over and above the exchange price, logistics costs of moving a product from point A to point B, warehousing costs, finance costs, credit costs, insurance costs, and so on. If you are hedging your physical deals, it is a trader's job to sell metal at a higher premium than they are buying it at.

For example, a trader is buying aluminum in Europe from a producer free on board (FOB) Rotterdam at $100/mt premium to the LME price, and their final sale is delivered duty paid (DDP) Baltimore, US. They would have various costs to move that metal from FOB Rotterdam to DDP Baltimore, such as vessel freight, finance costs, insurance, port handling charges at the destination, trucking costs in Baltimore, and so on. If these additional costs from FOB Rotterdam to DDP Baltimore, US, total to

$150/mt, their breakeven sales premium would be $250/mt. If they sell at a lower premium than $250/mt they will lose money; if they sell at a higher premium than $250/mt, they will make money. Table 5 below shows an example of this trade generating $3,300 gross profit, or $33/mt.

Table 5

	mt	$/mt	Premium	Ocean Freight	CIF-DDP Cost	Vessel Insurance	Finance Cost	Cash Flow
Physical Purchase	100	$2,000	$100	$70	$66	$2	$12	$(225,000)
Futures Sale	-100	$2,000	-	$ -	$ -	$ -	$ -	$200,000
Physical Sale	-100	$1,800	$283	$ -	$ -	$ -	$ -	$208,300
Futures Purchase	100	$1,800	$ -	$ -	$ -	$ -	$ -	$(180,000)
								$3,300

Concentrates

Concentrates trading utilizes **treatment charges** and **refining charges** to generate profits, instead of premiums. Treatment and refining charges are discounts to exchange-set prices commanded by consumers of concentrates in order to process the raw materials. In markets where metal concentrates are deemed scarce, treatment charges tend to be low because consumers (smelters) of the raw materials have less options to source material. If metal concentrates are deemed plentiful, treatment charges tend to be high because consumers have more options, so they can command a higher discount in order to process them. It is a trader's job to try and buy concentrates at a higher treatment/refining charge (discount) than they sell to consumers.

Table 6 below shows an example of a copper concentrates deal, with purchase and sale CIF Shanghai. Using a purchase TC of $100/dmt and an RC of $0.10/lb contained copper, and a sales TC of $90/dmt and an

RC of $0.09/lb contained copper, they are making gross profit of $107,831.

Table 6

	mt (8% moisture, 25% Cu @ 96.5% Payable)	$/mt	TC ($/dmt)	RC ($/lb contained copper)	Supervision & Assay Cost ($/dmt)	Cash Flow
Physical Purchase	10,000	$8,000	$100	$0.10	$1.50	-$16,360,485
Futures Sale	-2,225	$8,000	-	-	-	$17,800,000
Physical Sale	-10,000	$9,000	$90	$0.09	$1.50	$18,693,316
Futures Purchase	2,225	$9,000	-	-	-	-$20,025,000
						$107,831

Concentrates trading, maybe more so than other types of metal trading, also generates significant additional profits from manipulating quotational periods, differences in payable percentages, and trading spreads. We will discuss quotational periods and spread trading in particular in later chapters.

Scrap

Scrap metal is similar to concentrates in that it will trade at a discount to the LME price for that metal. It could be in terms of a percentage, such as scrap that trades basis a percent of the exchange set price, or it could be an outright discount in $/mt or cents/lb. Traders will try to buy scrap metal at either a lower percentage or larger discount in $/mt or cents/lb than they sell the metal at.

Table 7 shows an example of a trader buying 1000mt of brass copper at 57.5 percent of the LME basis FOB Guayaquil, Ecuador, and selling that brass at 60 percent of the LME basis CIF Shanghai. With costs from FOB to CIF totalling $122/mt, they are making a gross profit of $73,000.

Table 7

	mt	$/mt	Payable Percentage	Ocean Freight	Vessel Insurance	Finance Cost	Cash Flow
Physical Purchase	1,000	$8,000	57.50%	$80	$2	$40	-$4,722,000
Futures Sale	-575	$8,000		$ -	$ -	$ -	$4,600,000
Physical Sale	-1,000	$7,800	60.00%	$ -	$ -	$ -	$4,680,000
Futures Purchase	575	$7,800		$ -	$ -	$ -	-$4,485,000
							$73,000

It should be noted that the profit margins traders make on premiums, discounts, or treatment charges are gross profits, not net profits. Companies will still have a number of other costs they will need to consider when considering a trade's profitability. If a trade has a gross profit of 0.5 percent but the company's cost of doing business is 1 percent (salaries, other overheads, etc.), that trade may not be worth it as it would actually be losing money on a net basis. That said, sometimes companies will still choose to trade at smaller margins to grow their footprint in a marketplace or to grow relationships with key customers.

It is not just traders who utilize hedging. Miners who have a known cost of production can use forward hedging to lock in profit margins for future production. If a copper miner has a cost of production of $6,000/mt of copper contained, to produce 100,000wmt copper concentrate with 25 percent copper content, they can sell futures contracts to lock in the margin on that production. As detailed in Table 8, if copper is trading at $8,000/mt and they sell futures contracts at that level for the next year, they have essentially captured a $2,000/dmt gross margin on that production, even if the price of copper decreases to $7,000/mt by the time they sell their copper concentrate.

Table 8

	100,000 wmt (8% moisture, 25% Cu @ 96.5% Payable)	Cost of Production	Cash Flow
Mine Production	22,200	$6,000	$(133,200,000)
Futures Sale	-22,200	$8,000	$177,600,000
Physical Sale	-22,200	$7,000	$155,400,000
Futures Purchase	22,200	$7,000	$(155,400,000)
			$44,400,000

Take a consumer of refined aluminum. They have all of their other input costs to make their finished product, and they know that their breakeven cost to produce this product would be to purchase 100 mt of aluminum at $2,500/mt; below this they will make gross profit, and above this level they will take a loss. Aluminum is trading at $2,200/mt so they purchase aluminum futures to lock in that margin. If the aluminum price increases above their breakeven cost by the time they purchase the physical aluminum, their margin will be protected as long as they hedged correctly, as shown in Table 9.

Table 9

	mt	$/mt	Cash Flow
Finished Product Sale (contained aluminum)	-100	$2,500	$250,000
Futures Purchase	100	$2,200	$(220,000)
Physical Purchase	-100	$2,700	$(270,000)
Futures Sale	100	$2,700	$270,000
			$30,000

There are countless examples of different types of metal companies that use hedging, both for protection against price movements, and to lock in profit margins. Be it producers, consumers, miners, trading companies, large companies or small, their long-term success or failure often comes down to how well they manage their exposure to prices that are outside their control.

Chapter Summary

- Regardless of the method used to fix the price of a physical contract, to correctly hedge you will take futures action over the same time period.
- As shown in Table 1, when used correctly, hedging can mitigate losses caused by changes in the price of a commodity between physical purchase and physical sale.
- Contracts that are based on percentage payables need to be hedged based on those percentages, not the gross tonnage of the physical contracts. Table 3 details the correct hedging of a percentage-based contract. Hedging the gross tonnage of a percentage payable contract will create price exposure, as shown in Table 4, potentially leading to large losses.
- Refined metal traders generate profit and loss (P&L) through differences in the premiums over exchange prices between purchase and sale, as shown in Table 5.
- Concentrate metal traders generate P&L through differences in treatment charges and refining charges between purchase and sale, as shown in Table 6.
- Scrap metal traders generate P&L through differences in the discounts to exchange prices between purchase and sale, as shown in Table 7.
- Hedging is not utilized only by trading companies. It can be used by any company with an exposure to metals prices, such as miners, metal producers, and end consumers, as seen in Tables 8 and 9.

5. The Perfect Hedge

If your company hedges, you have probably heard the phrase "**Perfect Hedge**". When someone references this, they do not mean that a hedge they did was amazing and they are so proud of it! What a perfect hedge means is that the physical metal was hedged and futures contracts were executed for the **exact same volume as the physical deal,** down to the last kilogram, at the same price as the physical contract was fixed, thus eliminating all price risk from that contract. Companies often say they perfectly hedge their physical metal, but in reality this is not possible. Hedging can only get us so close to being perfectly hedged.

Futures contracts trade in set quantities. LME contracts on base metals trade in quantities of exactly 25 mt (copper, ali, lead, zinc), 20 mt (aluminum alloy and nasaac), 10 mt (steel), 6 mt (nickel), 5 mt (tin), and 1 mt (cobalt). On the CME, copper trades in 25,000-lb lot sizes (or 11.34 mt for those of you on the metric system). Aluminum, lead, and zinc trade in 25 mt lots, and cobalt trades in 2204.62-lb lots (equal to 1 mt). This means you can only buy or sell futures contracts in multiples of those lot sizes. If you have a physical zinc purchase for a contractual volume of 100 mt, the chances of you actually receiving exactly 100 mt are zero. You might receive 99.985 mt, but it still won't be exactly 100 mt. Most refined base metals contracts have a standard tolerance of 2 percent built into them. So for every 100 mt of physical metal you buy, the supplier is able to supply any amount from 98 mt up to 102 mt.

The issue here is that if you buy exactly 98.235 mt physical zinc but sell 100 mt zinc futures, you have technically hedged too much zinc by a total of 1.765 mt. Let's say between buying your physical and selling your physical, the price of zinc moves from $2,500/mt to $3,000/mt. When you buy back your futures short and sell your physical metal, you will be exposed on those 1.765 mt to the price difference. As shown in Table 10, in this case you would lose $500/mt on 1.765 mt or $882.50 total.

Table 10

	mt	$/mt	Cash Flow
Physical Purchase	98.235	$2,500.00	$(245,587.50)
Futures Sale	-100	$2,500.00	$250,000
Physical Sale	-98.235	$3,000.00	$294,705
Futures Purchase	100	$3,000.00	$(300,000)
			$(882.50)

Luckily, most companies aren't only trading 100 mt of a commodity. The way most companies handle the small differences between futures exchange contract volumes and physical volumes is to run a hedge card for each metal that pools all of the company's priced positions together. A hedge card is a report, usually run daily, that compares all of the physical sales and purchases that have been priced, against all of the futures shorts and longs the company has executed. This will generate a net number of the company's exposure. The company works to keep this net number within half a lot of zero, positive or negative. Once their exposure exceeds half a lot from a net-zero position, they can square themselves by either buying one lot or selling one lot.

The aim of the perfect hedge is to stay as close as possible to a net-zero exposure, which is managed daily. Table 11 shows a very rudimentary example of a hedge card. Your company may use something similar, or they may have a much more detailed system, but the main goal will be the same: to show the net priced exposure for the company between all of the priced physical and the hedged futures.

Table 11

LME COPPER	Physical Contracts	mt
	P-XXXXXX	99.560
	P-XXXXXX	350.000
	P-XXXXXX	124.588
	P-XXXXXX	1,007.844
	P-XXXXXX	234.180
	P-XXXXXX	75.000
	P-XXXXXX	203.457
	P-XXXXXX	52.300
	P-XXXXXX	850.000
	P-XXXXXX	97.676
	P-XXXXXX	201.299
	S-XXXXXX	-1,000.000
	S-XXXXXX	-234.180
	S-XXXXXX	-300.000
	S-XXXXXX	-650.000
	S-XXXXXX	-52.300
	S-XXXXXX	-97.676
	S-XXXXXX	-200.000
	S-XXXXXX	-100.000
	Physical Total	**661.748**
	Net Futures	**-650.00**
	NET POSITION	**11.75**

Note that some of the priced contracts are round numbers, which indicates they haven't been fully delivered against yet, so final tonnages are not known. Some of the purchases and sales have the same tonnages. This indicates they are allocated to each other and the operator has done a good job in amending the contracts to their **final weights**. Table 11 shows a physical total priced position of 661.748 mt, and a net futures position of -650 mt. This gives you a net copper exposure of long 11.75 mt. No action would be needed because the company is less than half a lot away from a net-zero position. If over the course of their trading they became more than 12.50 mt exposed, then they could sell one lot of copper futures to bring their exposure back within half a lot of zero. On the other hand, if they were showing an exposure of short more than 12.5 mt, they would look to buy one lot of copper futures to bring their exposure within half a lot of zero.

Another common question is regarding contracts that price over an **average**, whether that is a partial average or a full monthly average. For example, you have a 100 mt physical lead purchase and you have agreed with your customer to fix the price of this over the average cash settlement price of a given month that has 20 pricing days in it. To hedge this perfectly, you would have to sell 5 mt of futures on the cash settlement of each of those 20 pricing days. Given lead trades in lot sizes of 25 mt, it is not possible to sell only 5 mt per day. However, your 100 mt sell order for lead is not the only one the broker you use on the LME to hedge your material will receive. The brokers are able to offer the ability to hedge any number of lots over an average because they will take it into their net position. LME brokers will be receiving requests to fix thousands of tons over the average each month, so it is easy for them to let customers hedge four, seven, ten, etc. lots because the impact on their overall position will be negligible. You can rest assured that your 5 mt/day is being hedged accordingly.

Chapter Summary

- Companies will often use the phrase 'perfect hedge', making the assumption that their physical contracts are hedged to the exact same tonnage at the exact same price.
- Because base metals futures trade in fixed lot sizes that don't perfectly match the tonnages of their physical shipments, a perfect hedge is not fully achievable, and a small exposure is inevitable, as shown in Table 10.
- Trading firms manage this exposure using a hedge card, an example of which is shown in Table 11. The hedge card combines all physical shipments for each metal and compares that position to the combined futures position for each metal, giving a net exposure.
- Companies will try to keep their net exposures within a half lot of zero at all times.
- If an exposure exceeds this limit, they will either buy or sell one lot to bring them back within half a lot of zero.
- Companies are able to hedge small lot sizes correctly over full or partial month averages as brokers combine all of their client positions large and small to create their own net position and accommodate your averaging requests.

6. Position Management

Up to this point, when I've referenced buying or selling a futures contract, I deliberately wanted to keep things simple and hence have done so without talking in depth about prompt dates. It is important for you to understand the principle of hedging first without getting bogged down in too much terminology and positioning. However, position management is almost as important as the act of hedging itself, so it is worth spending some time familiarizing yourself with this aspect of hedging and how it is applicable to your job.

A prompt date is the date on which your futures contract settles. As mentioned in Chapter 3, the LME is unique compared to most markets in that you can buy or sell a futures contract that will be prompt any business day. CME metal futures are only prompt the last business day of the month, whereas you could have an LME position prompt any business day of the month. However, the most liquid day of the month for LME contracts is the **third Wednesday** of each month-this means the highest volume of trades will be prompt this day each month. Because of this, a lot of companies will keep all of their hedges prompt the third Wednesday of each month because they are much easier to manage than having positions prompt on random/sporadic days throughout the month. If you are trading an LME contract basis a month, such as selling ten lots of December LME copper, what that actually means is you are selling ten lots of copper that is prompt the third Wednesday in December.

Why the third Wednesday? The LME chose the third Wednesday of each month because there was no UK or US bank holiday that would ever fall on that date. Because the exchange settles in US dollars, it needs both the UK and US markets to be open. However, in 2021 the US officially made June 19th of each year a federal holiday, commemorating the end of slavery in the US (June 19th 1865). This now means that there will be sporadic years where the third Wednesday of June is a US bank holiday. When this occurs, no warrant deliveries or pickups will be able to be made on June 19th, with deliveries resuming on June 20th. After the deadline of 'tom' rolling on Tuesday June 18th, any open, unsquared futures positions will be automatically rolled from June 19th to June 20th at level (zero cost or gain) using the previous day's settlement prices.

The LME and CME are physically settled exchanges. If you let a futures trade become prompt on the LME or CME, you will either take delivery of physical metal if you have bought futures, or you will be obliged to deliver physical metal if you have sold futures, of an LME/CME-approved brand to a LME/CME approved warehouse.

Most of the time, you do not want to let a position become prompt and have to receive/deliver metal to the LME or CME. Let's say you bought some physical copper that you planned to sell in December. When you hedged this physical purchase, you placed your futures short in December accordingly - meaning that hedge sits on the third Wednesday of December. Now, let's say something happens that causes a delay in shipping that purchase. In order to not be left with a futures **short position** that would create an obligation to deliver metal to the LME, we move this short position. For positions on the CME, your long or short position can be called upon as soon as the first business day of the prompt month it sits in. Because of this, CME positions should be moved at the latest by the last business day of the month prior to the prompt month. The type of trade that moves a futures position is called a **carry** trade.

There are two types of carry trades, a **borrow** and a **lend**. Anytime you are buying a nearby date and selling a date further into the future, that is called a borrow. And when you are selling a nearby date and buying a date further into the future, this is called a lend. In the above example in which your physical purchase was delayed, you would have to buy December third Wednesday futures to square your December short position, and sell January third Wednesday futures so you are now short January. When you execute a borrow or a lend, you are executing both the buy and the sell trades at the same time. If you did not execute these two trades simultaneously, you would be creating outright price risk by going long or short that commodity.

Table 12 shows your square December position from the original shipment schedule. Table 13 shows the carry trade required due to the delay in shipment from December to January.

Table 12

Original Schedule	December
Physical Purchase	100
Futures Sale	-100
	0

Table 13

Shipment Delayed	December	January
Physical Purchase		100
Futures Sale	-100	
Borrow	100	-100
	0	0

The highlighted cells above show your carry trade, a borrow in this case because you have bought December futures and sold January. Your physical is now square against your futures in January, and you no longer have a futures position in December.

If it were the case that instead of a physical purchase being delayed a physical sale was brought forward, you would need to lend, as shown in Tables 14 and 15.

Table 14

Original Schedule	January
Physical Purchase	100
Futures Sale	-100
Physical Sale	-100
Futures Purchase	100
	0

Table 15

Sale Brought Forward	December	January
Physical Purchase	100	
Futures Sale		-100
Physical Sale	-100	
Futures Purchase	100	
Lend	-100	100
	0	0

The highlighted cells show your carry trade. You originally placed your physical purchase hedge in January because that's where you believed your physical sale was going to take place. You have sold December futures and bought January futures to square your position in both months.

As discussed, both on LME and CME, there will usually be a difference in price quoted for each prompt date of the commodity you are trading. The differences in these prices create what is known as the **forward curve**. These forward curves determine the level of your carry trade and, importantly, whether there will be a cost or a gain to your P&L resulting from it.

If prices are increasing with time between prompt dates, that market is in a **contango**. For example, if the December price for copper is quoted at $8,000/mt and the January price for copper is quoted at $8,010/mt, then it is said the December-January market for copper is in a $10/mt contango. If, on the other hand, prices are decreasing with time between prompt dates, then that market is in a **backwardation**. If the December price for copper is quoted at $8,010/mt and the January price is quoted at $8,000/mt, then it is said the December-January market for copper is in a $10/mt backwardation. The collective term used for the difference in price between two prompt dates is called the spread (carry trades are also often called spread trades).

If you are borrowing, you want to be doing so at a time when the price is higher in the future. You are buying nearby and selling further out, so you want to be paying a lower price than you are selling at. Conversely, if you are lending, you are selling nearby and buying further out so you want to be doing so when the nearby price is higher than the further out price. A quick way to remember this if you are struggling is the three Bs: **B**orrowing in a **B**ack is **B**ad. Since lending is the opposite of borrowing, as long as you can remember the three Bs, you can work out the other three scenarios: borrowing in a contango is good, lending in a back is good, and lending in a contango is bad.

In Tables 16 through 19 you will find examples of carry trades and their respective cash flows for borrows and lends in contango and backwardations.

Table 16

Borrow in a Contango	January	$/mt	February	$/mt	Cash Flow
Physical Purchase	1,000	$2,500			$(2,500,000)
Futures Sale	-1,000	$2,500			$2,500,000
Physical Sale			-1,000	$2,300	$2,300,000
Futures Purchase			1,000	$2,300	$(2,300,000)
Borrow	1,000	$2,400	-1000	$2,415	$15,000
					$15,000

In the above example, you needed to move your physical purchase hedge from January to February to match it to your physical sale pricing month. At the time of the borrow, the price for January aluminum was $2,400 and February was $2,415, a contango of $15/mt, so the carry trade generated $15,000.

Table 17

Borrow in a Backwardation	January	$/mt	February	$/mt	Cash Flow
Physical Purchase	1,000	$2,500			$(2,500,000)
Futures Sale	-1,000	$2,500			$2,500,000
Physical Sale			-1,000	$2,300	$2,300,000
Futures Purchase			1,000	$2,300	$(2,300,000)
Borrow	1,000	$2,415	-1,000	$2,400	$(15,000)
					$(15,000)

The opposite is true for borrowing in a backwardation. The January price for aluminum was $2,415 at the time of the carry trade vs. a February price of $2,400. You bought at the higher price and sold at the lower price, so the carry trade here has cost $15,000.

Table 18

Lending in a Backwardation	January	$/mt	February	$/mt	Cash Flow
Physical Purchase			1,000	$2,500	$(2,500,000)
Futures Sale			-1,000	$2,500	$2,500,000
Physical Sale	-1,000	$2,300			$2,300,000
Futures Purchase	1,000	$2,300			$(2,300,000)
Lend	-1,000	$2,415	1,000	$2,400	$15,000
					$15,000

Here, you are moving your physical purchase hedge from February to January. You are selling nearby and buying further out, so you are lending. Because there is a backwardation and the January price is higher than the February price ($2,415 vs. $2,400), the carry trade has generated $15,000.

Table 19

Lending in a Contango	January	$/mt	February	$/mt	Cash Flow
Physical Purchase			1,000	$2,500	$(2,500,000)
Futures Sale			-1,000	$2,500	$2,500,000
Physical Sale	-1,000	$2,300			$2,300,000
Futures Purchase	1,000	$2,300			$(2,300,000)
Lend	-1,000	$2,400	1,000	$2,415	$(15,000)
					$(15,000)

The opposite is true if you are lending in a contango. The January price here was $2,400 and the February price $2,415. You are selling at a lower price and buying at a higher price, so the carry trade here has cost $15,000.

Many different factors influence the forward curve. In general, if a market veers into a backwardation, it is deemed that supply is tight nearby. People are willing to pay more to get metal now than they are in the future. The opposite is usually true when the market is in a contango because it is deemed plenty of material is available now, so why would someone pay over and above what they would in the future when there may be less of the material available?

These are not hard and fast rules, and many factors can influence forward curves. Some are related to organic changes in supply and demand, and some are driven by market participants trying to move the market in certain directions, or caught with a position they need to get out of.

Forward curves can be impacted suddenly and sometimes even without good reason, or at least not an obvious one.

It's important to note that forward curves are by no means linear. I have never seen a forward curve with a perfect 45-degree angle that just keeps going up and up with time to infinity. Even in a healthy contango market, we usually see a tapering of the curve after a few months, in large part because liquidity is much better within the three-month trading period. A market may also be in a contango for parts or even most of the curve with sporadic months of backwardation. Markets can also be in backwardation for the entirety of the curve, or contango for the front half of the curve that tightens into a backwardation in the back half. There is no set pattern for a forward curve, so you cannot rely on patterns being consistent.

In Charts 1 and 2 you will find examples of the forward LME copper curve that use real-life data from two different dates, just two weeks apart in October 2021. Notice how the shape of the curve differs between charts, illustrating just how varied forward curves can be, how quickly they can change, and how drastic the changes can be.

Chart 1

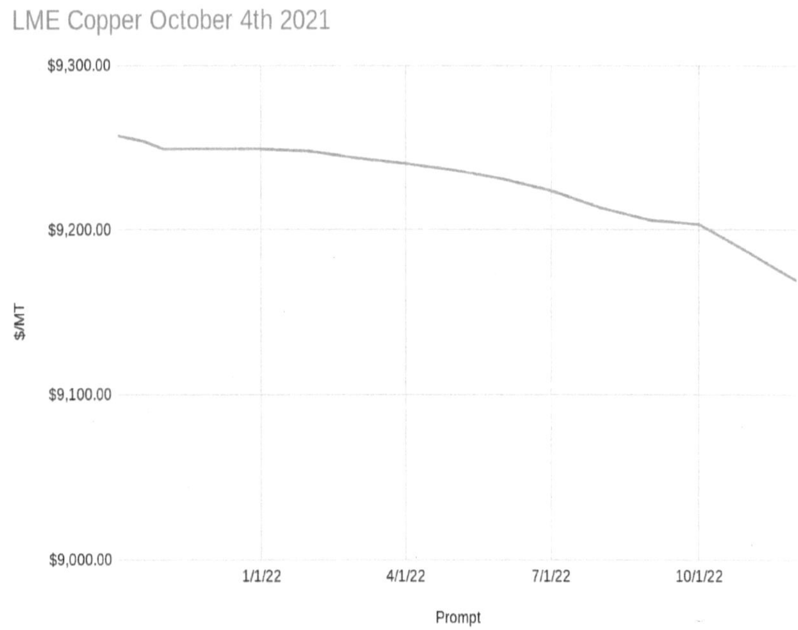

In Chart 1, while copper is in a backwardation all through 2022, the curve is relatively shallow and then begins to get steeper toward the end of 2022. In Chart 2 on the following page, only two weeks later, the backwardation in the nearby months has grown incredibly steep to over $1,000/mt. After the initial month, it remains relatively shallow with time through the end of 2022. A company not properly managing their spread exposure that needed to borrow a futures short position through this cash to 3's period, would have faced a cost of over $1,000/mt for that carry trade.

Chart 2

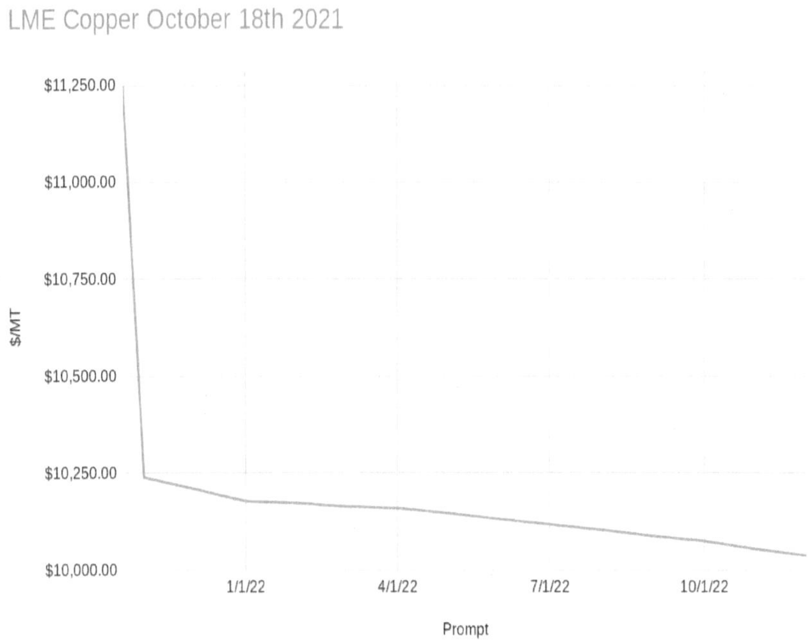

Contangos are, in general, capped at **full finance**. Metal costs a set amount to finance based on the price of that metal and the interest rates banks charge you to borrow money. In addition to the cost of finance is the cost of LME or CME rent a warehouse charges you to store the metal. These two costs added together will be your cost to hold the metal month over month, often called your carry cost. If a month-to-month contango were to become larger than this full finance cost, you could in theory borrow at a higher contango than your carry costs, buy as many LME or CME warrants as you wanted, and get a risk-free return. Typically, the closer a contango gets to full finance, the more it will be borrowed, so the spread will begin reducing from full finance as demand for the trade increases. Some companies that hold metal in non-LME storage pay significantly lower rent rates compared to those charged by LME warehouses. Their cost of carry is much less than holding LME warrants, and they are often able to generate profits using this technique.

Backwardations, on the other hand, can be much higher than full finance. The LME has changed their rules on how big a backwardation can be for what's known as tom-next trading, where you need to move a position that is prompt tomorrow (tom) to the day after. But there is no cap on month-to-month spreads. Given trading firms are often physically long before they sell material, they are naturally short futures. A real risk to a physical trader is not managing their spreads correctly and getting caught in a big backwardation they have no choice but to borrow through. This can easily negate any potential profit they would have made on a trade.

You may have heard the terms **tightening** or **easing** and not known what that means when it comes to spreads. If a market or certain spread is tightening, it either means a contango is shrinking or a backwardation is getting larger. The opposite is true for easing-this means that a contango is getting larger or a backwardation is shrinking. I am a visual learner, so when I was first learning about spreads, I liked to imagine a line with zero in the middle (see Figure 1). To the right are positive numbers (contango) 1, 2, 3, . . . infinity, and to the left are negative numbers (backwardation), -1, -2, -3, . . . -infinity:

Figure 1

BACKWARDATION													CONTANGO											
-∞	...	-10	-9	-8	-7	-6	-5	-4	-3	-2	-1	0	1	2	3	4	5	6	7	8	9	10	...	∞

If the market is tightening, we are moving from right to left on the above figure. If a spread is in a $10 contango and it moves to the left to a $5 contango, it has tightened by $5/mt. The same is true if it was in a $5 backwardation and it moves to a $10 backwardation; we are still moving to the left, so we are seeing spreads tighten.

If the market is easing, we are moving from left to right. If a spread is at $10 backwardation and it moves to $5 backwardation, then it has eased by $5/mt. The same is true if we were in a $5 contango and the spread moves to a $10 contango; we are moving to the right, so we are seeing spreads ease.

Importantly for your work, you must remember that forward curves are fairly sporadic in nature and they can and do change day to day. An operator who keeps a keen eye on spreads will be much more valuable to their company than one who has no idea about these prices and makes decisions (or fails to make decisions) that can cause losses instead of making proactive choices to earn or save the company money.

For simplicity in understanding the principles of hedging and position management, I have made the assumption that in your day-to-day work you will be required to manage your positions on a third-Wednesday-to-third-Wednesday basis. However, it is worth mentioning that companies trading on the LME don't exclusively keep their positions on third Wednesdays.

If you buy or sell a futures contract basis cash, or on the cash settlement price, that future, unless adjusted, would be prompt two business days from the day you trade it. Three month trades are prompt three months (to the nearest business day) from the date of execution. Monthly average trades on the LME are prompt two business days after the last business day of the month. Trades that are not prompt on a third Wednesday can be managed in a variety of ways; there is no requirement for companies to manage their positions on a third-Wednesday-to-third-Wednesday basis.

Most companies that trade basis cash, or on monthly averaging will have those trades adjusted to a third Wednesday when they place the trade. For example, let's say it is the first business day of January, and you are pricing a physical sale with your customer on today's LME cash settlement price. Here, your hedge would be buying futures on the same day's LME cash settlement price. In order to have that trade be prompt the third Wednesday, the request would be placed with your broker to buy January (third Wednesday) futures **basis** that day's cash settlement price. What you are doing here is making two trades: buying futures prompt two business days time, and then lending them to the third Wednesday (you are selling nearby to square your cash position and buying third Wednesday). In practice, you never see the carry trade; your broker simply fills you with a **long position** on the third Wednesday, using the forward curve at the time to calculate the third Wednesday price. If you were selling futures instead of buying them, the process is the same, but your carry trade occurring in the background would be a borrow.

If instead you had agreed to price your physical sale over the average of the whole month of January, your hedge would be buying futures on each day's cash settlement. This would eventually give you a long position prompt the second business day of February. Obviously, your cash trade each day of the month would not naturally be prompt on the second business day of February. Monthly average trades consist of buying or selling each day's cash settlement, then carry trades, moving each of those cash positions to the second business day of the following month. From your perspective, you will still only see one hedge, but the price quoted to you by your broker for executing the average trade will be inclusive of all of these small carry trades.

In order to have your average January futures purchase be prompt the third Wednesday of January, you will require a carry trade to move that long position back to the third Wednesday. You would be borrowing from the third wednesday of January to the second business day of February. This would square your long position on the second business day of February and establish your long position where you wanted it on the third Wednesday of January. This trade is called a month-on-month average trade (in this case, January-on-January). Brokers will quote these average trades as the cost or gain of the carry trades involved. If you were selling futures on the average instead of buying them, then the process would be the same, only your carry trade to establish the third Wednesday prompt would be a lend.

It should be noted that when hedging over the average of a month, January for example, you may not want to move that hedge to the third Wednesday of January but to the third Wednesday of a different month. This is common in concentrates trading. If you have a physical purchase with an average January pricing but know the sale this parcel is allocated to is pricing over the average of April, you can adjust your average January trade to be prompt the third Wednesday of April. Because you are buying physical, you would be selling futures on the average of

January, which means you would be short futures prompt the second business day of February. The carry trade would therefore be borrowing that short position from the second business day of February, to the third Wednesday of April. This trade is often referred to as an average borrow. On the other hand, if you were pricing a physical sale over the average of January and wanted that resulting long futures position to be prompt the third Wednesday of April, you would be lending the second business day in February to the third Wednesday of April, often referred to as an average lend.

As mentioned above, companies are under no obligation to keep their LME futures positions exclusively on third Wednesdays. You may have heard people at your company (particularly larger trading firms) discussing tom-next trading (tomorrow to the next business day) or holding cash positions (trades prompt in two business days). In these scenarios, they deliberately keep nearby positions and enter into repeated one-day or other very short-term carry trades in order to try and gain additional profit. However, these types of trading decisions are almost always made by traders. If you are discussing tom-next trading regularly, I'm going to assume my work on this particular chapter is done and you are fairly competent in the basics of position management!

Chapter Summary

- Position management is extremely important to the profitability of commodity companies.
- LME futures can have prompt dates on any business day of the month. CME futures only have prompt dates on the last business day of the month.
- The third Wednesday of each month is the most liquid prompt date for LME trading. Because of this, companies often manage their futures positions on a third-Wednesday-to-third-Wednesday basis.
- The LME and CME are physically settled exchanges, which means a futures position that is left to become prompt will become an obligation to take delivery of metal (if you hold a long position) or an obligation to deliver metal to the exchange (if you hold a short position).
- To avoid futures positions becoming physical obligations, they are moved using carry trades-borrowing and lending.
- Borrowing is buying a nearby prompt and selling a prompt further in the future, as shown in Table 13.
- Lending is selling a nearby prompt and buying a prompt further in the future, as shown in Table 15.
- The profitability of a carry trade is determined by the forward curve. If prices are increasing with time, that market is said to be in contango. If prices are decreasing with time, that market is said to be in backwardation.
- Forward curves are rarely linear and can change quickly and drastically in value. Charts 1 and 2 provide real-life examples of the LME copper forward curve only two weeks apart, showing how significant these changes can be.
- If a market is easing, it means a contango is getting larger or a backwardation is getting smaller (moving from left to right in Figure 1).
- If a market is tightening, it means a contango is getting smaller or a backwardation is getting larger (moving from right to left in Figure 1).

- Companies are not under any obligation to keep their positions on third Wednesdays. Larger commodity firms will often try to extract additional profits by trading tom or cash positions on a daily basis.
- If requested, brokers will adjust cash and average trades to third Wednesdays without the need for separate carry trades. They will fill you with one futures trade that is prompt the third Wednesday of the requested month. The price will differ from the cash price, and the broker will use the forward curve to calculate the third Wednesday value.

7. Physical Shipments

Hopefully you now have a good understanding of the basic principles of hedging. It is time to look at exactly how this forms part of your day-to-day responsibilities. It is important to remember how your actions can have a direct impact on the hedging decisions your company makes. Often, hedging is viewed as just prices on a screen, something that occurs in the background, not influenced by the middle or back office. The reality is that once a trader has booked a trade, so many of the decisions that can impact hedging are made by operators, schedulers, and other non-trading roles.

A term you need to be familiar with is **quotational period (QP)**. When a trader books a trade, they will define in the trade confirmation and contract exactly when and how that trade will be priced; this is the quotational period. While it probably won't be part of your role to decide on the QP, it is often part of your role to set up the hedging for the contract. Therefore, you need to know by heart the QPs for the shipments you are managing.

A few definitions are worth getting used to given they are common in the industry:

- **Unknown Price**: The price will be set at an as yet undefined date in the future.
- **Fixed Price**: The price has already been fixed at the time of entering into the contract.
- **Average Price**: The price will be set over the average of a given number of days, which could be a full month(s) or partial month average.
- **M**: M is the term given to the scheduled month of shipment. It is used in conjunction with how the contract will price. For example, the average cash settlement price of M would mean the average cash settlement price over the scheduled month of shipment.
- **M-1/M-2/M-3**: Where M means scheduled month of shipment, putting a minus sign after M signals prior, so M-1 would be one

month prior to scheduled month of shipment, M-2 would be two months prior to scheduled month of shipment, and so on.

- **M+1/M+2/M+3**: Where M means scheduled month of shipment, putting a plus sign after M signals after, so M+1 would be one month after scheduled month of shipment, M+2 would be two months after scheduled month of shipment, and so on.
- **MOAS**: Month of Actual Shipment. Some contracts will call for a price to be fixed not just on the scheduled month of shipment, but on the actual month of shipment based on bill of lading (BL) dates (the date a vessel sails).
- **MOAS +/-**: Same as when using M, plus and minus can also be added to MOAS to define prior or after.
- **Official Cash Settlement Price (LME)**: The official cash offer price set by the LME during the second ring.
- **Lowest of the Fours (LME)**: The lowest official price set by the LME during the second ring between cash bid, cash offer, 3M bid, and 3M offer.
- **Market on Close (LME)**: The official closing kerb price posted by the LME.
- **TAS (CME)**: The daily settlement price posted by the CME.

QPs can be defined as in the **buyer's option**, the **seller's option**, or **mutually agreed**, depending on the specific contract.

An important part of managing your contracts should be sending pricing confirmations to your counterparties prior to the start of a QP. Often, a long time can pass between a trader sending a trade confirmation or signing a contract and actually buying or selling the material. It is industry standard and good practice to send QP declarations. It serves not only as a reminder both internally and to the counterparty as to how the price will be set, but having a paper trail regarding the hedging you are undertaking can prove extremely important in the case of a dispute. You are reconfirming your intent to price per the contractual terms, or you are confirming a change from the contractual terms before the contract is to start pricing. Either way, the counterparty has been given a chance to challenge you if they believe you are mistaken. Without QP confirmations, things can get messy if a customer believes you have fixed the price incorrectly. You are also much less likely to forget to hedge something or send incorrect hedging instructions internally if you have sent a QP confirmation to the customer. Any changes to QPs must always be fully documented for the same reasons as above, regardless of whether they occur before or after a QP has started.

Often, you will send a pricing confirmation for an unknown pricing. You may be in a situation where you are nearing the end of a QP and a customer has not yet fixed the price of a contract. Conversations should be ongoing internally surrounding contracts that have not yet priced in their scheduled QP month. Anytime you have to move a QP, there may be a carry trade involved. Managing unpriced contracts before the end of a QP allows more time for your team to take appropriate trading action before you are forced into it.

Sometimes your physical contracts may have something called QP optionality built into them. A QP option means one of the counterparties involved in the contract has the option to amend or redefine the QP up to a specified date. This could be a spread option, where, for example, a contract can price either M or M+3, declared before the start of M. This is called a spread option because you are able to capture the spread between the QP option months if it is in your favor. It could be a pricing option where, for example, the contract could price over the average of M-1 or M, declarable at the end of M-1. Often this is called a back-pricing because you are able to declare what price the contract will take after one of the QP options is already known.

These QP options can be simple or complex, but either way they are often profitable. Where you will need to pay close attention is to the declaration dates in your contracts. Although traders are making the decisions as to which QP option you will be declaring, it will often be the operators who actually declare the QP option to the counterparty. Failure to declare on time can be disastrous. Not only can you jeopardize the profitability of the QP option, but you may end up with a price (and therefore hedge position) your counterparty disagrees with.

QPs are often linked to the shipment dates of your physical contracts. Operators are often the first to see delays or changes to shipment schedules. Delays to shipments are commonplace in the commodities industry, but if delays occur, it is important to raise the issue to traders so they can address any changes to hedging that may be required, regardless of whether that shipment is priced or un-priced. You should also update shipment dates in your system as soon as changes to schedules are known. Hedge cards often draw their data directly from the system you use, so if physical contracts are sitting in the wrong delivery months, incorrect data may be used to make trading decisions.

Another extremely important but often overlooked aspect of your shipments and how they relate to hedging is updating provisional tonnages to final tonnages once they are known. Contracts are usually booked in round numbers, such as 100, 200, or 500 mt. In reality, contracts are not round numbers. Much like shipping schedules, operators are typically the first ones to know the final weights of a contract. The larger the contract, the larger the variance from a round or perfectly hedgeable tonnage you may end up with. As soon as you have the final weight for a contract, it is your job to update your system to reflect the accurate tonnage. If you have a physical copper purchase contract for 1,000 mt and the final weight comes in at 975.875 mt, but you have hedged 1,000 mt then you are 1 lot or 25 mt overhedged. This doesn't mean you hedged incorrectly initially, but if you do nothing, your system will not know that you are overhedged by 25 mt, so no one will know to buy back the one lot you are overhedged by. The quicker you can update tonnages from round numbers to their final weights, the lower the chance you will incur a hedge loss from the resulting over or under hedge.

Table 20

Update Final Tonnage as Soon as Possible	mt	$/mt	Cash Flow
Physical Purchase	975.102	$8,000	$(7,800,816)
Futures Sale	-1,000	$8,000	$8,000,000
Futures Purchase	25	$8,025	$(200,625)
			$(1,441)

Table 21

Waits a Month to Update Final Tonnage	mt	$/mt	Cash Flow
Physical Purchase	975.102	$8,000	$(7,800,816)
Futures Sale	-1,000	$8,000	$8,000,000
Futures Purchase	25	$9,500	$(237,500)
			$(38,316)

As you can see in Tables 20 and 21, when the final tonnage was updated quickly, there was only a $25/mt difference between the original hedge price and the hedge correction, so the loss was minimal. When the operator waited a month to update the tonnage, the market had moved significantly higher, and the cost of waiting to correct the hedge on only a one lot correction was $38,316.

Updating tonnages is not limited to refined metals contracts. Percentage-based contracts such as concentrates or scrap deals are often hedged using provisional percentages, even if the exact tonnage of the shipment is known. These percentages are then to be adjusted once final **assays** are received back from internationally accredited laboratories and agreed upon by buyer and seller.

For example, if you have a 10,000wmt copper concentrates shipment you have agreed to buy at 25 percent copper contained using provisional assays, at a 96.5 percent payable, and 8% moisture, initially you would hedge 2,225 mt of copper, or 89 lots. If upon receiving final assays the actual copper content was 24 percent, even though that's only a change of 1 percent, that means that the correct amount of copper you should have hedged is 2,125 mt or 85 lots. In this case, you have sold four lots too many. If left unchecked, your overhedge of four lots would continue to create an exposure. The longer this exposure remains, the larger the corresponding hedge loss could be. Concentrates shipments are often much higher tonnages than refined metal shipments, so even small percentage changes in final versus provisional assays can have significant consequences when it comes to hedging. It is just as important to update final percentages on these contracts as it is final tonnages.

The best middle and back office employees I have worked with are the ones who were acutely aware how their day-to-day actions impacted hedging and hence had the potential to affect P&L. They were therefore meticulously accurate and proactive in the management of their contracts.

Chapter Summary

- Decisions made by middle and back-office employees can have a significant impact on the hedging process.
- The QP defines exactly how and when a physical contract will be priced. They can be in the buyer's option, the seller's option, or mutually agreed. You should become familiar with the terminology used in QPs.
- Pricing confirmations serve as a reminder both to your counterparty and internally as to how a physical contract will be priced, and therefore hedged. They provide a paper trail in case of a dispute. Any change to QPs must always be fully documented and conveyed to all relevant parties.
- You must pay extremely close attention to contracts that have declaration dates in the QP.
- Operators are often the first to know of changes to physical shipment schedules. It is important to alert traders to any changes to shipment schedules as soon as you become aware of them. You must also make sure any systems you operate in are kept up to date so contracts are not sitting in the wrong delivery months.
- It is vitally important to update physical contracts in the system once final tonnages are known. Waiting to do so can create unnecessary losses, as shown in Tables 20 and 21.
- Equally important is updating final percentages on contracts that are based on payables. Even small changes in final assay percentages can create large exposures that if left unchecked can cause large losses.

8. How to Become a P&L Generator

Not to sound like a broken record, but being in a middle or back office function does not mean you are simply there to move product from point A to point B. There are real opportunities for you to increase profits by taking some simple steps in your day-to day-work. At minimum, you can save the company from making unnecessary losses. However, if you are absent-minded about these decisions, they can easily lead to unintentional losses. I do want to point out that even if you are confident that an action will lead to additional profits or prevent a loss, you should always check with your manager/trader before taking action by yourself. It is much better to raise an idea first, discuss it, and get approval to move ahead than to act independently.

The industry standard tolerance in weight for physical metal contracts is 2 percent, but 3 percent is not uncommon. I have even had contracts that allowed a 10 percent tonnage tolerance from the contractual volume. These tolerances are in place for reasons already mentioned; it is nearly impossible to achieve round numbers in final weights. If you have a 500 mt sale, the odds of ending up with a final weight of exactly 500 mt are zero. These allowed tolerances create an opportunity for you in either over, or under-shipping a contract. The larger the contract tonnage, the larger the opportunity.

Operators are typically in charge of shipping schedules, choosing which parcels of stock to ship, and when to ship them. Let's use a 1,000 mt aluminum contract with a 3 percent tonnage tolerance that has been fully priced at $2,500/mt. You have arranged shipment to be completed evenly throughout the month, shipping a few trucks per day. The last week of the scheduled delivery month arrives and you have completed approximately 900 mt of the 1,000 mt delivery. Because you have been following the aluminum price, you notice that the price has decreased since you fixed the price of the contract, and is now $2,000/mt. If you add one extra truck to this delivery to take the total weight to approximately 1,025 mt, you would no longer be perfectly hedged.

You initially bought 40 lots of aluminum at the same $2,500/mt that you agreed for the physical sale. However, if you deliver 1,025 mt, then to remain perfectly hedged, you would need to buy one additional lot of aluminum futures. The customer would still be paying the contractual price of $2,500/mt for the extra truck, but you are able to hedge that extra truck at the lower price of $2,000/mt. As shown in Table 22, the net result of your proactive decision-making is a gain of 25 mt multiplied by the difference between the hedge price for the additional lot, and the customer price, in this case, $2,500 - $2,000 = $500/mt * 25 = $12,500. By the simple act of shipping one extra truck, you have increased the $/mt profitability of the entire trade by $12/mt.

Table 22

	mt	$/mt	Cash Flow
Physical Sale	-1,000	$2,500	$2,500,000
Physical Sale Over-Shipment	-25	$2,500	$62,500
Futures Purchase Hedge	1,000	$2,500	$(2,500,000)
Over-Shipment Futures Purchase	25	$2,000	$(50,000)
			$12,500

This opportunity is also present if instead of the price decreasing after it has been fixed, it increases from $2,500/mt to $3,000/mt. However, instead of delivering an extra truck, you would under-deliver by one truck and finish the contract at 975 mt instead of 1,000 mt. Having originally bought 40 lots to hedge this contract, you would now be over-hedged by one lot and can sell that lot back at the higher price of $3,000/mt. Table 23 shows the net result of your under-shipping is $3,000 - $2,500 = $500/mt * 25 = $12,500. You were able to achieve the same additional profit as if the price had decreased simply by paying attention to the aluminum price, being aware of the details of your contract, and closely managing your shipping schedule.

Table 23

	mt	$/mt	Cash Flow
Physical Sale	-975	$2,500	$2,437,500
Original Futures Purchase Hedge	1,000	$2,500	$(2,500,000)
Under-Shipment Futures Sale	-25	$3,000	$75,000
			$12,500

While there are opportunities to create profits, if you fail to pay attention to shipment weights, you could just as easily create losses. If you fail to keep an eye on these details, you could accidentally overship a sale when the price increases or under-ship a sale when the price decreases.

Let's say you operate in a country where truck weight limits are 25 mt. For a 1,000 mt sale, you book 40 trucks. The warehouse only loads each truck to around 24.5 mt. After shipping 40 trucks, your total weight delivered is 975 mt. Some operators don't think to check the details. They assume deliveries are complete and move on to the next contract. In doing so, they are unaware the aluminum price has decreased, and their under-shipping has just cost the company money when it's time to adjust their hedge, as shown in Table 24.

Table 24

	mt	$/mt	Cash Flow
Physical Sale	-975	$2,500	$2,437,500
Original Futures Purchase Hedge	1,000	$2,500	$(2,500,000)
Under-Shipment Futures Sale	-25	$2,000	$50,000
			$(12,500)

In this case, you should ask the warehouse to send one more truck, to get you closer to the original 1,000 mt contractual tonnage-and probably have a serious talk with the warehouse about why they were not loading trucks to capacity! If the situation allows, you may even try to overship by one truck.

The important thing to remember is that regardless of which direction the price has moved, once you have fixed the price of a contract, there are potential opportunities to create profits through the actions you take. At bare minimum, it is incumbent on you to pay close attention to final shipped weights and compare them to the contractual/hedged tonnage to limit any hedge loss.

It is not always as simple as making these decisions internally; you must also consider the counterparty. If the scenario is one where under-shipping a sale would bring additional profits but your customer is desperate for the material, it may not be prudent to under-ship them. Or if over-shipping would be beneficial but the counterparty is maxed out on capacity and wouldn't want the extra load, shipping additional material would probably cause an issue. I cannot stress enough that customer relationships are by far the most important part of physical commodity trading. A short-term gain for you that ruins a relationship with a long-term customer is not a wise move. Provided the consumer is not clamoring after every last ton, these opportunities are usually acceptable.
The consumer is not the only consideration here, which is why internal discussions with your team are always necessary. There may be a $100/mt backwardation that you would have to pay if you under-shipped because it creates a need to borrow additional tonnage you'd have to hold in stock an additional month. If you are making $50/mt from the hedge gain, it doesn't make sense to under-ship. If you are facing financing pressure because it's a quarter/half/year-end, your company may wish to forego the hedge gain in order to reduce their stock position. When you make these suggestions, come armed with all the necessary knowledge. For example, we will be making $X/mt on the hedge gain, the customer doesn't need the metal, there's a healthy contango so it won't hurt us carrying the stock, etc.

There is less opportunity to take advantage of this on physical purchases because you are not in charge of the shipping, so you cannot control final weights yourself. However, you can still pay attention to the price and the tonnages as you receive them. If the seller lets you know they are finished with their deliveries and they have under-shipped, you can quickly work out if this would be a hedge gain or loss. If it would be a loss, discuss as usual internally. If it makes sense, check with the supplier to see if they can ship an additional truck to bring you closer to contractual weights. Conversely, if based on a supplier's shipping schedule you see they will end up overshipping, the procedure is the same: work out whether, based on the contractual price compared to the current market price, if this would be a hedge gain or a loss. If a loss, speak to the supplier and let them know that sending that last truck isn't required. These requests may not be granted, but not asking and just leaving it up to chance is taking unnecessary risk.

Another opportunity that often presents itself is regarding QPs for unpriced contracts. Delaying pricing to a following month or bringing forward pricing can often depend on when material is shipped. You have a sale but know your customer is full to the brim with material. Being the excellent operator that you are, you have developed a fantastic relationship with your counterparty's team, and they are happy to share this information with you! Because you have been paying attention to spreads, you also know that there is a very wide contango of $16/mt right now. Delaying shipment to the customer would allow you to borrow your short position to the next month and gain the $16/mt. Because you know your cost of finance is $5/mt/month, and your non-LME rent is $3/mt/month, you would be gaining $8/mt simply by delaying shipment and moving the QP.

Similarly, if you know there is a large backwardation, you can call up one of your customers who you have a feeling is desperate for material. If your suspicions are confirmed, speak with your trader, who can enquire if the counterparty would be happy to bring the QP forward and accept delivery a month early. Your proactivity in bringing this information forward has at minimum saved your company the cost of the backwardation. In the best case scenario, if they were already borrowed through it, they can now lend the position back one month to actually gain the value of backwardation.

Opportunities for profits can be even larger on contracts that are already priced. Take a 500 mt copper sale that has been priced on the first day of the month at $8,000/mt. This metal is supposed to be delivered the second week of the month, but your counterpart calls you and lets you know they are having consumption issues and won't be able to take delivery until the following month. Since you fixed the price of this contract, the copper price has risen to $8,500/mt. If you share this information with your trader as soon as you find out, they may be able to request a change in QP to the following month, when you will actually deliver the material. If the trader can successfully renegotiate the QP, you would need to sell back your original hedge, which was a 500 mt long position at $8,000/mt. You would sell 500 mt to flatten your position (also known as unwinding a hedge) at $8,500/mt, and make $500/mt, or $250,000. If you wait a few days or weeks before letting the trader know shipment is delayed, they are much less likely to be able to request a change in QP. End consumers who don't hedge their material are often open to these types of changes.

Counterparties will often call you as the first point of contact to request a change related to shipping. Maybe it's a request to reduce or increase a contractual tonnage. It could be changing the month of delivery and therefore a QP month. If you are following your markets closely and looking for opportunities, you can create win-win scenarios that seem to the customer that you are going above and beyond for them. You may well be, but you are also generating profit for your company. Although you always want to be able to assist a request from a counterparty, you don't want to say yes to all requests without considering the hedge implications that result from them. It is easy to create a hedge loss without realizing it if you aren't paying attention. It is extremely important to discuss any requests you receive from a counterparty with your trader before responding.

In my experience, I have found that a lot of physical consumers are willing to accept small (and sometimes large) changes to shipments, QPs, or outright prices if there is a justifiable reason. It could be that they are making a finished product where the impact of a change in the price of the metal you are delivering will have a negligible impact on their overall cost.

A $50/mt change in 200 mt of zinc you are delivering may be of no concern to them, but an additional $50/mt profit to you on those 200 mt could be doubling your profit margin. Some consumers are so large that there is a lot of flexibility in shipping dates or volumes. For some, the LME price of the metal is just a pass-through to the consumer of their final product. Often physical metal consumers are not hedging the metal they are buying for a number of reasons (some justified and some misguided), so there can be a lot of leeway with the price of your delivery.

Opportunities for hedge gains are always presenting themselves if you are looking for them. Even if your company doesn't end up capitalizing on a suggestion, the fact you are bringing these ideas forward will show that you have commercial understanding. If you do want your career path to eventually move to the front office, it is these kinds of ideas that your company will be looking for when assessing who is ready for a commercial role.

Chapter Summary

- Opportunities for middle-office functions to create hedge profits occur daily. At worst, you will be able to prevent unnecessary hedge losses on your contracts.
- It is extremely important to always check ideas with your manager and trader before acting on them.
- Tolerances on physical contracts provide opportunities for over or under-shipping. The larger the contractual tonnage, the larger the opportunity.
- By keenly managing your shipping schedules, knowing your contract prices, and knowing current market prices, you have the ability to create hedge gains. Tables 22 and 23 show examples of over and under-shipping to create additional hedge profits.
- Failing to pay attention to over and under-shipping can just as easily cause hedge losses, as shown in Table 24.
- When making these decisions, the counterparty's needs and the long-term relationships must come first. There is no point making a quick hedge gain at the cost of a customer relationship. However, in my experience, physical consumers are often flexible.
- When considering P&L opportunities, you must also keep in mind other factors such as subsequent carry trades that would be required and financing pressures.
- Despite not being in control of purchase shipping schedules, you should still pay close attention to prevent losses.
- QP adjustments based on changes to shipping schedules can provide additional opportunities for profits.
- Always discuss changes requested directly to you by counterparties with your trader before responding.

9. Hedging Errors

No matter how good you are at your job, you will inevitably make a mistake. The commodities industry is an extremely fast-paced environment. You will be handling multiple contracts simultaneously, and even the most organized, detailed-oriented employees will eventually make a misstep. There is nothing to be ashamed about in making a mistake, and they can provide great learning opportunities. As long as you handle it appropriately, they can actually have a positive impact on your career in the long run. My first week on the deals desk, I sold an option contract instead of buying one; it cost the desk $60,000. I've never made the same mistake again, in large part because of how I handled the situation.

The most important thing you can do if you realize you have made an error when it comes to hedging is **immediately** raise it to your manager and your trader. It could be that you forgot to send a hedge request, or you bought futures instead of sold them, or you miscalculated the tonnage and hedged the wrong number of lots. Whatever the mistake is, the quicker you raise it, the easier it will be to rectify without a loss. The longer you wait to fix a hedging error, the greater the chance of a large loss. Commodity prices are volatile-a daily price range of more than 3% is not uncommon, so even leaving something for one day longer than you have to, can have devastating consequences if you are on the wrong side of the trade.

Discuss what happened with the relevant people to try to understand what you did that caused the error. Was it simple oversight? Do you need a concept explained more thoroughly? Do you need help with your workload? What actions are needed to correct the hedge? Discuss what the result of the error will be. Sod's Law-or Murphy's law, depending on your geographical location-dictates that hedge errors seem to lose money 9 out of 10 times when they are corrected. Once these conversations have taken place, and actions have been taken to fix the error, take a minute to reflect on what you will take away from the experience. Be humble, and know that because of the error, you have learned a valuable lesson that you will strive to not repeat.

I have never seen someone be fired for making a simple, honest mistake when it comes to hedging. I have, however, seen multiple people fired for making a mistake and trying to hide it, or moving past it, thinking it was not a big deal (which it might not have been if they had tried to correct it properly immediately). Or, and this is probably the worst one, finding an error that would result in a loss, and thinking they could time the market and wait for the price to change to dig themselves out of a hole. Waiting to deal with a hedge error will inevitably lead to this conversation with your superior:

“When did this happen? Two weeks ago?! To correct the hedge at that time, the price was only $30/mt out of the money, and now it is going to cost us $500/mt!”

Unfortunately, that is often followed by a trip to human resources and a swift exit from the building, which could all be avoided. Handling errors correctly will prevent this situation occurring and drastically reduce the chance of making similar errors again.

Chapter Summary

- Making a mistake in your role is inevitable.
- Provided you handle mistakes correctly, they can provide great learning opportunities.
- Immediately raise errors to your manager and trader. The longer you wait to discuss the situation, the higher the chance of a large loss.
- Make sure you review what the cause of the error was, and understand what you did, or didn't do correctly.
- Never try to time the market before fixing an error.

10. Warrants

In prior chapters, you learned why position management is such an important aspect of hedging. As discussed in Chapter 6, in almost all cases you would not let a futures position become prompt. However, because the LME and CME are physically backed exchanges, they can be used as both a source of material and a delivery point for material. On occasion, physical consumers, producers, or traders will take advantage of this and use the exchanges to either buy metal from or deliver metal to.

LME

Except for steel contracts, every lot that is traded on the LME is backed by a physical warrant. A warrant is a physical parcel of metal in an exchange-approved warehouse, of an exchange-approved brand. The tonnages of warrants must be within two percent (higher or lower) of the size of the futures contracts: 25 mt (aluminum, copper, lead, zinc), 20 mt (aluminum alloy, nasaac), 6 mt (nickel), 5 mt (tin), or 1 mt (cobalt). If you are long one lot of copper futures and allow that long position to become prompt without lending it, you will be delivered 25 mt (+/- 2 percent) of an LME-approved brand of copper, in an LME warehouse somewhere in the world. Similarly, if you are short one lot of copper futures and allow that short position to become prompt without borrowing it, you will be obligated to deliver 25 mt of an LME-approved brand of copper, to an LME warehouse of your choice.

The LME keeps an updated list of all of their approved warehouses globally along with all of the approved brands of metal. Provided metal meets the chemical specifications that the LME has defined as acceptable for delivery, any amount of metal produced by those approved branded producers can be delivered onto warrant.

When you are buying warrants, most of the time you do not want to be delivered a random brand of metal without knowing exactly where you will be receiving it. The holders of warrants are actively trading them between one another or to traders or end consumers of that material. Buyers of warrants will typically pay a premium to the holder of the warrant to guarantee a certain brand or a certain location for their material. It is usually at this point they would establish their futures long position, or let their existing futures length become prompt, because they know what metal they will be delivered and where. Once you have been delivered your warrants and they have been paid for, you will issue cancelation instructions to the LME warehouse. By sending cancellation instructions, the material will be removed from the LME system and will no longer be an LME warrant. At that stage, it will simply be physical material in an LME warehouse, ready for physical consumption.

For larger traders, another option is **sifting** warrants. If you know there are specific warrants available, either brand or location, but you don't want to pay a premium for them, sifting can be a good option. It is called sifting because a trader will typically pick up a very large number of warrants, so they are casting a large net. Although they will receive a lot of material that doesn't necessarily interest them, they will also hopefully be delivered some material they actually want. For example, a trader may get long 1,000+ lots of aluminum by borrowing the position. That means that they will be long nearby and when that 1,000-lot long position becomes prompt, they will be delivered 25,000 mt of aluminum. When the warrants are delivered to you, you receive the list of all of the brands and locations you have received. The trader quickly reviews this list (or sifts through), identifies any warrants they want to keep, and then starts the process of delivering back the warrants they don't want. To do this they simply establish a short position by lending. This creates a short position to deliver the warrants they don't need, and squares out the short position created from the initial borrow. If you are quick enough in your decisions, this can all be effected the same day you receive the warrants and delivered back the following day (tom). Sifting is not without risks-if the spread changes too much between putting on the initial borrow and lending to deliver the unwanted warrants back, you risk paying out more on the carry trade than you would have in premium to just select the warrants you wanted. You also have to pay rent, and finance costs on all of the material until you can deliver it back. Sifting is a calculated risk, and traders will work to mitigate those risks as best they can.

Traders and producers also utilize the LME as a delivery point for metal. Sometimes market conditions may make deliveries to the LME profitable. Provided you own an LME-approved brand metal in an LME-approved warehouse, you will be able to deliver material onto the LME exchange by creating warrants. Once the metal is in an LME-approved warehouse and lotted up into 25 mt (+/- 2 percent) parcels, you would send instructions to the warehouse to create the warrants and deliver them to the broker you have established your short futures position with. There is no limit as to how much metal can be delivered onto the exchange, provided it meets the exchange set specifications for brand, analysis, and location.

There could be many reasons someone would want to deliver metal onto the LME. There could be a large backwardation, and if you have a short position, you would have to borrow through that backwardation, costing you money. Instead, you could deliver metal against that short, saving the cost of the borrow. Or, a trader may actually capitalize on a backwardation and create a short because they have excess metal and their position is already borrowed past the backwardation. By lending into the backwardation, they aren't just saving the cost, they are creating P&L.

A company may be holding a large amount of stock and want to reduce these holdings but the physical demand for that product in the consumer market is weak at that time. Provided the metal meets specifications, the LME would provide an immediate delivery point to sell that metal into.

Warehouse companies themselves may also incentivize deliveries into their warehouses. LME warrants earn warehouses a predetermined daily rent. There are also set fees for load-out charges upon cancellation of metal. Warehouse companies can calculate the time they believe metal will remain in their warehouse and pay incentives to producers or traders to deliver metal to them. If the local premiums in the physical consumer market are comparable or even less than the incentive a warehouse is offering, you may see metal flow onto the LME instead of being physically consumed. While LME warehouses themselves are prohibited from owning LME warrants, they can still have an influence on the warrant market.

CME

Most of the details regarding CME warrants are the same as on the LME. Paying a premium for specific warrants in specific locations, establishing long or short positions to receive warrants or deliver warrants to the exchange, and reasons for delivering warrants onto the exchange are all still applicable for CME warrants. However, there are some differences.

Every lot traded on the CME is also backed by a physical warrant, but CME copper trades in lot sizes of 25,000 lbs, so CME copper warrants are considerably smaller than LME warrants. CME aluminum, lead, and zinc warrants are 25 mt parcels, the same as on the LME. The CME also keeps an updated list of CME-eligible warehouses and CME-eligible brands of metal, but for CME copper, their warehouses are only in the US. So if you are long or short a CME copper future and it becomes prompt, you would either need to deliver or be delivered metal in the US. The CME warehouse locations for aluminum, lead, and zinc extend to Europe and Asia.

Because of the prompt date structure of the CME, sifting for CME warrants is possible, but it looks a bit different than sifting on the LME. You would still establish a large long position in the month you wanted to buy warrants. But because there is only one prompt date per month, you have much less control over whether your particular long positions will be called for delivery each day of that month. The closer you get to the end of the month, the more likely your long positions will be delivered against, but you cannot plan for the exact delivery dates like you can on the LME. Once you have taken delivery of your warrants, the process for either canceling the metal and using it for physical consumption or delivering the warrants back to the exchange is essentially the same as it is on the LME.

Chapter Summary

- The LME and CME are physically backed exchanges. This means that producers, consumers, and traders can utilize the exchanges as sources of metal and delivery points for metal.
- To buy warrants or deliver warrants, you first need a futures position in the month you wish to buy or deliver. Instead of moving this futures position with a carry trade, you would allow it to become prompt. If you are long futures, you will be delivered metal; if you are short futures, you will be delivering metal into the exchange.
- Warrants are only located in and can only be delivered into specific LME-and CME-registered warehouses. The metal held as warrants in these warehouses is guaranteed to meet a certain LME or CME chemical specification, and be produced by LME-and CME-registered producers.
- Premiums are paid to secure specific brands of metal or warrants in specific global locations.
- Sifting is a method of finding highly sought-after warrants without paying a premium for them.
- Periods of backwardation often provide opportunities for deliveries into the exchanges as traders look to profit by lending their positions into the backwardation.
- While they are not able to actually hold warrants themselves, warehouse companies may incentivize deliveries into their warehouse if they believe they can make more than the incentive they pay in load-out fees and warehouse rent.
- CME copper is held exclusively in warehouses in the US.

11. Arbitrage

In simple terms **arbitrage**, or arb, is the simultaneous buying and selling of a commodity to exploit price differences in two different markets for that same commodity. While arbitrage is often used to generate profits-and entire divisions of companies can be dedicated to speculative arbitrage positions-it is also utilized as a method of risk mitigation.

There are many different markets and commodities this occurs in. Here, I will be talking about the arbitrage between CME and LME copper contracts. While they are closely linked, the price for LME copper is set independently from the price for CME copper, and because of this, there is inevitably a difference in price between the two.

Domestically in the US, almost the entire copper market is priced using CME prices. Globally, however, the majority of copper outside of China is traded using the LME as the price setting mechanism. Domestic US consumers or traders of copper who source their material from the rest of the world (ROW) will need to establish positions (enter into futures contracts) on both CME and the LME. Similarly, domestic US producers of copper or traders who export from the US to ROW will also need to establish positions on both CME and the LME.

Let's look at a scenario for each of the above situations. A trader is buying copper cathode in Africa with the aim to import it into the US to sell to a copper consumer. When they buy the material, they will create a short position on the LME to hedge their purchase. When they sell the metal to the US consumer, they will create a long position on the CME to hedge their sale. As shown in Table 25, although they have a square futures position tonnage wise (they are long the same number of futures as they are short), they are still exposed because those futures positions are held on different exchanges. Remember, CME copper trades in lot sizes of 25,000 lbs (equivalent to 11.34 mt), so there will still be a very small mismatch between the two exchanges, but this is to some extent unavoidable.

Table 25

	mt	LME	CME
Physical Purchase	1,000		
Futures Sale		-1,000	
Physical Sale	-1,000		
Futures Purchase			997.92
	0	**-1,000**	**997.92**

In order to square their positions, they would need to put on an arb trade, whereby they buy LME copper and sell CME copper. They would now be square in terms of tonnage, and also eliminate their exposure on both exchanges. This trade is detailed in Table 26 below.

Table 26

	mt	LME	CME
Physical Purchase	1,000		
Futures Sale		-1,000	
Physical Sale	-1,000		
Futures Purchase			997.92
Arb Trade		1,000	-997.92
	0	**0**	**0**

The opposite trade would need to be established if, instead of importing LME-priced copper to the US, you were exporting CME-priced copper to the ROW and pricing your sale on the LME. If you bought copper from a domestic US producer that priced the metal using the CME, you would create a short position on the CME. When you sold this material to your customer in Europe, you would create a long position on the LME, as shown in Table 27.

Table 27

	mt	LME	CME
Physical Purchase	1,000		
Futures Sale			-997.92
Physical Sale	-1,000		
Futures Purchase		1,000	
	0	**1,000**	**-997.92**

Just as the importer of LME copper to the US was not square across exchanges, neither is the exporter. In order for the exporter to square their positions, they would need to buy CME copper and sell LME copper, as shown in Table 28.

Table 28

	mt	LME	CME
Physical Purchase	1,000		
Futures Sale			-997.92
Physical Sale	-1,000		
Futures Purchase		1,000	
Arb Trade		-1,000	997.92
	0	**0**	**0**

Typically, traders will not simply wait until they hedge their purchases or sales to put on the arb required for their hedging. In tables 25 through 28, I did not include the prices that were involved in executing the arb trades. They were merely examples of the directional trades you would have to execute in each market to square your position. If your arb trade is to buy CME futures and sell LME futures, you want to try to do so at a time when the LME is trading at a higher price to the CME. Conversely, if your arb trade is buying LME and selling CME, you want to put on that arb when the CME is trading at a higher price than the LME.

Table 29

	mt	LME	CME	$/mt	Cash Flow
Physical LME Purchase	1,000			$7,500	$(7,500,000)
Futures Sale		-1,000		$7,500	$7,500,000
Physical CME Sale	-1,000			$7,000	$7,000,000
Futures Purchase			997.92	$7,000	$(6,985,440)
LME Futures Purchase		1,000		$7,300	$(7,300,000)
CME Futures Sale			-997.92	$7,350	$7,334,712
		0	0		$49,272

In Table 29, the trader put on the arb trade when the CME copper contract was trading at a $50/mt premium to the LME copper contract. They have locked in that margin between the two contracts. Even if the arb reverses (or flips) and LME copper moves to trade at a premium to CME copper, you have squared your position and are no longer at risk.

If you know (or have a good idea of) the timing of your forward purchases, sales, and the months their QPs will be in, you can establish your arb trades needed to square your positions at any point before actually fixing the price with your customer. Your company may actually wish to enter into arb trades before they have even made physical purchases or sales if they know they will need a certain amount of arb trades executed per month and the market is in their favor.

Just like matching physical purchase and sales QPs by month, you will also need to match your arb positions to the physical QP months. If your physical sales QP is in March, then that is the prompt month you will need to execute your arb trades in. If you don't, you will be creating another exposure, not negating one.

The price differentials between LME copper and CME copper are changing all the time, sometimes drastically day by day, hour by hour, or even minute by minute. Companies often have whole teams dedicated to identifying the most opportune times to execute arb trades to generate additional profit for the company, or at least limit the losses from the difference in prices between markets.

From a middle office perspective, the important thing to remember is that arb is necessary to eliminate the price exposure created when buying and selling physical metal that prices on two different exchanges. If you do not eliminate this risk, not only will you have unsquared futures positions on different markets that will become prompt (and, as discussed, these are physically backed markets, so this would create a physical obligation), but you will have a constantly changing price exposure created by the difference in price between the two exchanges. This changing price exposure could easily negate any profit from the trade unless it is mitigated.

Chapter Summary

- Arbitrage, or arb as it is commonly known, is the simultaneous buying and selling of the same commodity across two different exchanges.
- If you are trading physical metal across two different exchanges, arb becomes an important risk mitigation tool as well as a method of generating additional profits.
- If pricing a physical purchase on one exchange and a physical sale on another, without an arb trade, you will still have open futures positions on each of those exchanges, even though your combined futures position may be flat, as shown in Table 25.
- Table 26 details an example of an arb trade required to flatten the futures positions when pricing a physical copper purchase on the LME and the equivalent physical copper sale on the CME.
- Traders usually execute arb trades in advance of hedging their physical purchases and sales, provided they have a good idea of when and how much arb is required.
- Arbitrage rates are constantly changing, and traders will try to execute arb trades at the most opportune and profitable times. Table 29 gives an example of a trader locking in an arb trade that generates $50/mt profit.
- The prompt months of arb trades must be matched with the QPs of the physical shipments otherwise, exposures will not be mitigated properly.

12. Premium Hedging

Traders who hedge their outright price exposure on refined metals make their profits from the difference in premium between their purchases and sales. In 2012, the CME launched premium contracts for the midwest US premium, followed in 2015 with their Rotterdam duty paid and duty unpaid premiums, and in 2016 launched contracts for the CIF Japan aluminum premium. These contracts allow traders of aluminum products to also hedge their exposure to premiums. This doesn't mean that traders who utilize this market aren't making any money on their premiums, but it offers them a way to lock in forward premiums and guarantee margin. While premium contracts are (at the time of writing) nowhere near as liquid as base metal outrights, they are traded in enough volume that most traders can utilize them for hedging purposes.

Premiums for physical aluminum contracts in the US, Europe, and certain parts of Asia, are often agreed to using a premium set by a publication. For the US, this is the Platts Aluminum MW US Transaction premium, and it is quoted in US cents/lb. For Japan this is the Platts CIF Japan Spot Premium for Aluminum, and it is quoted in US dollars/mt. For Europe, this is the Metal Bulletin Aluminum P1020A, in-whs Rotterdam Duty Paid and Duty Unpaid premiums, and they are quoted in US dollars/mt. Each day, these publications discuss current spot market premiums with traders, producers, and consumers in order to set the daily premium for their respective markets. Buyers and sellers of metal agree in advance to use whatever the premium that is set by these publications for their contracts. For example, in January you could agree to buy 1,000mt of aluminum from a producer, to be delivered in March, at a premium to be defined by the Platts average daily premium for the month of March. This is called a floating premium purchase or sale. These types of contracts are commonplace, but they do come with risk. You are agreeing to buy or sell material at a premium to the LME, but you don't know what that premium is going to be. This is where the ability to hedge that premium risk comes into play.

The CME Premium contracts themselves are swap contracts, with one leg linked to the above publication daily premiums for each of the respective markets. They are the same tonnage size as the aluminum contracts that trade on the CME & LME: 25 mt. What this means, is that if you are selling ten lots of December US Midwest DDP Premium futures contracts at 25 cents/lb, you are also agreeing to buy ten lots at whatever the Platts Midwest December average premium is at the time of publication.

How exactly does this help mitigate premium risk? Let's say you are long 1,000 mt of physical aluminum that you bought from a producer at a fixed premium of 20 cents/lb. The metal won't be delivered to you for another month, but as luck would have it, the aluminum market has tightened since you bought at 20 cents/lb, and premiums have gone up to 25 cents/lb. Your sale is pricing over the following month's Platts average. If you take no action on the CME, you are at risk of the market cooling and your profit decreasing from the 5 cents/lb you would get on today's spot market (25 cents spot sales minus your 20 cent purchase premium). To prevent this from happening, you enter into a CME premium sale at 25 cents. Per above, this means that you are agreeing to sell at 25 cents, and buy at whatever the following month's Platts average ends up being. Essentially, you have converted your physical sale premium from an unknown number (the following month's average) into a fixed sale at 25 cents. The four trades you have transacted are shown in Table 30 below. Even if the premium for the following month crashes to 17 cents/lb, you are still making your 5 cents/lb margin:

Table 30

Fixed Premium Purchase	mt	Premium (cents/lb)	Cash Flow
Physical Purchase Fixed Premium	1,000	$0.20	$(440,924.00)
Physical Sale Floating Premium	-1,000	$0.17	$374,785.40
Premium Swap Fixed Sale	-1,000	$0.25	$551,155.00
Premium Swap Floating Purchase	1,000	$0.17	$(374,785.40)
			$110,231.00

Your profit is locked in between the CME fixed sale and your fixed premium physical purchase. Your physical sale is perfectly offset against the second leg of the CME swap, where you are buying over the same average premium as your physical sale. Typically, traders will enter into this type of contract if they think that the market is peaking and don't want to risk premiums falling. They may also be happy with the current margin they could make using CME Premium contracts and not want to take the risk premiums could decrease. Similar to outright price hedging, your upside is also capped in this scenario. If premiums actually carried on increasing, you would not see any of that upside. Remember, hedging is a risk mitigation tool. The risk here is that premiums will decrease, so you hedge to protect yourself against a move you have no control over.

The opposite trade would be entered into if you had sold physical metal at a fixed premium, and were buying your metal at a floating premium. Let's say you have sold at a $500/mt premium DDP Rotterdam. Since that sale, market premiums have decreased to $400/mt. You are buying your physical on the following month's Rotterdam DP average premium per Fastmarkets. You don't know how long the market is going to be depressed for, so you want to lock in your $100/mt margin. You enter into a CME premium purchase at $400/mt. You are agreeing to buy fixed at $400/mt and sell at whatever the following month's Fastmarkets

Rotterdam DP premium print ends up being. Here, you have converted your physical purchase premium from an unknown number into a fixed purchase at $400/mt, using the trades shown in Table 31.

Table 31

Fixed Premium Sale	mt	Premium ($/mt)	Cash Flow
Physical Purchase Floating Premium	1,000	$600	$(600,000)
Physical Sale Fixed Premium	-1,000	$500	$500,000
Premium Swap Floating Sale	-1,000	$600	$600,000
Premium Swap Fixed Purchase	1,000	$400	$(400,000)
			$100,000

Similar to the previous example, you have mitigated the risk of premiums increasing by the time you buy your physical purchase. Had premiums continued to fall, you have capped your profit at $100/mt, but when premiums moved up to $600/mt, you still made $100/mt compared to losing $100/mt had you taken no protective hedge action.

In order for this type of hedging to properly mitigate your risk of premium fluctuations, you should execute the forward swap in the same month that your unknown premium for your physical sale or purchase is going to price. If, for example, your physical sale is going to price in May but you sell an April premium swap, then you are not mitigating your sales premium risk. The price of the second leg of the swap, which will take the April average publication premium, will not necessarily be the same as the May average publication premium. You would still have an exposure to the difference between the April premium and the May premium that your physical sale is being priced at.

Chapter Summary

- For certain refined metal products such as aluminum, mitigating the fluctuations in premiums is possible by entering into forward premium swap contracts.
- It is common for physical aluminum contracts to be entered into at an unknown premium based on a premium set by a publication.
- If you are long physical aluminum at a fixed premium and think premiums may decrease before fixing the premium on your physical sale, you can sell a forward premium swap to lock in the current market premium. Table 30 shows an example of this trade.
- If you are short physical aluminum at a fixed premium and think premiums may increase before fixing the premium on your physical purchase, you can buy a forward premium swap to lock in the current market premium. Table 31 shows an example of this trade.
- Forward premium swaps should be executed in the same month as you will price the unknown premium on your physical purchase or sale.

13. Foreign Exchange Hedging

Most commodity companies report their financials in US dollars (USD). The LME and CME are both settled in USD. However, it is not uncommon to be required to transact with a counterparty in a currency other than USD, depending on the geographical locations you are buying or selling material. This creates a risk for companies that make purchases and sales in a currency that is different from the currency their own accounts are kept in. Fortunately, **foreign exchange (FX)** hedging can be used to mitigate your exposure to fluctuations in FX rates. A benefit of FX hedging compared to physical metal hedging, is that while the LME and CME have set lot sizes, you can hedge currency to the exact cent you need to. So if it suits, you can achieve a perfect hedge when it comes to currency hedging.

While the LME is settled in USD, they do publish FX rates daily that companies can agree to use to convert their LME prices into Great British pounds (GBP), Euros (EUR), and Japanese yen (JPY). This LME print is simply a reflection of the Reuters 1 p.m. daily fix; the LME does not actually print their own fix for FX. Companies do not have to use the rates that the LME publishes. Much like pricing metal, you can agree on various FX settlements, averages, or even use a live rate based on wherever spot rates are at the time you agree the price and FX rate with your customer.

If, for example, you have agreed to buy 100 mt of aluminum from a producer that conducts their business in euros, you will inevitably need to purchase euros to pay your supplier. If you do not handle that purchase of euros correctly, you could be creating a loss without realizing it. Let's say you agree to price your physical contract on tomorrow's LME cash settlement, and use the Reuter's 1 p.m. fix to convert the USD price into euros. This means you will need to buy euros at the same rate your customer is using to convert the LME price into euros. You would place an order to buy euros and sell USD for the USD value of your material, based on the LME cash settlement. If the CSP for aluminum is $2,200/mt that day, and the premium for that metal is $400/mt, then you would sell: 100 * ($2,200+$400) = $260,000 at the 1 p.m. Reuters fix. If the fix for EUR/USD that day was 1.05, you would have sold $260,000 and received

€247,619.05-this is the exact amount of euros your customer is expecting to be paid for the 100MT of aluminum.

If you neglected to hedge this FX exposure at the time of fixing the FX on the contract, you would still need to buy the euros to pay your supplier, because the contract was agreed to be fixed in euros.

Foreign currency exchange rates change by the second and are often as volatile in their movements as outright prices of base metals. Let's say you just bought euros on the day you needed to pay the supplier. This may be a number of days, weeks, or even months after fixing the price of the metal. On the day of payment, the EUR/USD rate has risen to 1.10. You have already fixed the EUR/USD rate with the customer at 1.05, so they are still expecting to receive €247,619.05. If you had hedged these euros correctly and bought them when the rate was 1.05, it would have cost you $260,000. However, since the rate has moved against you, buying the same 247,619.05 euros will now cost you $272,380.96. By not hedging the euros correctly, you have lost $12,380.96, or ~$124/mt in margin on your 100 mt aluminum purchase.

It is the same case on sales in a foreign currency. If your company keeps their accounts in USD, when selling material that prices in a foreign currency, you would need to convert that back into USD when you are paid. Let's say you have agreed to sell 200 mt of zinc at $3,000/mt plus a premium of $300/mt, and are using an FX rate of 1.04. Both the LME price and FX rate were fixed using live screen prices. Your customer is going to pay you 200 * ($3,000 + $300) = $660,000/1.04 = €634,615.38. To hedge this, you would have bought USD and sold euros at that same rate of 1.04. You are square on your euros position because the customer will pay you €634,615.38, and this is the amount that you sold. Because you sold at 1.04, you will still receive your expected $660,000.

If you hadn't taken any hedging action on the euro exposure, you will still need to sell the euros when your customer pays you for the material, then convert them into USD, as that is what your company's financials are based on. If the EUR/USD rate moves down to 1.00, you are only going to receive $634,615.38 when you convert those same €634,615.38 instead of the $660,000 you would have received had you sold the euros at the time of fixing the contract. Your loss by not hedging the euros correctly is $25,384.62, or ~$127/mt on your 200 mt zinc sale.

As mentioned above, FX hedging has the advantage of being much more precise than metal hedging. In both scenarios above, I have used round numbers for the tonnages. In reality, your final tonnage is going to be slightly different. This is why, similar to your base metals hedging, it is always vitally important to keep your systems updated as soon as you have the relevant information. If in the 100 mt aluminum purchase example you receive final weights and the contract tonnage is actually 98.455 mt, then you would have bought slightly too many euros. The contract was priced at $2,600/mt (including the premium), and so you sold $260,000 and bought €247,619.05. Based on the final weights, you should have only sold $255,983 and bought €243,793.33. In order to stay perfectly hedged, you will need to sell back €3,825.72. The quicker you can update the contract to the final weights, the less chance there is of the FX rate having moved drastically from the original rate.

You will have a similar issue if the contract final weight was higher than 100 mt. If it is actually 101.98 mt, then instead of needing to pay the supplier €247,619.05, you would need to pay them $2,600 * 101.98 = $265,148/1.05 = €252,521.91. You will need to buy an additional €4,902,86 to have enough euros to pay the supplier in full.

You may be thinking, it's only a few thousand euros that you are over-or under-hedged, so it wouldn't have that big of an impact, right? That's the wrong mindset. Every time you can save your company even a single dollar by making sure your contracts are accurate, you should do it. Additionally, most companies are not built on 100 mt deals. They are built on tens of thousands of tons, sometimes much more than that. If you multiply the above example of an over shipment by a factor of ten and change it to a 1,000 mt contract that had final weights of 1019.80 mt, now the exposure is €49,028.60, and that's just on one contract.

If you are neglecting to update your contracts to final tonnages and currencies are remaining over-or under-hedged, over time it will have a huge impact, not just on your company's bottom line, but also very likely on your career in commodities.

Chapter Summary

- Most commodity companies report their financials in USD, however it is not uncommon to transact in a currency other than USD (EUR, GBP, CHF, etc.).
- This creates a need to mitigate risks of fluctuations in FX rates, which can change just as quickly as base metals prices.
- There are many different ways to fix the FX rates on a physical contract, including published settlements and live screen prices.
- If you are buying physical metal in a non-USD currency, you will need to buy a set amount of that currency, and sell USD in order to pay your supplier.
- Failing to purchase that non-USD currency at the same rate you have agreed to fix with your supplier would create an exposure.
- Hedging that exposure properly involves buying the non-USD currency at the same time, and hence the same rate you agreed with your counterparty.
- The same is true for physical sales, only your hedge will be selling the non-USD currency and buying USD at the same time, and hence at the same rate you agreed with the counterparty.
- If desired, you can actually achieve a perfect hedge on FX exposure, down to the last cent.
- Updating your physical shipment quantities is equally important for FX hedging as it is for outright base metals hedging.

14. Spread Cards

In Chapter 5 we discussed how companies use simple hedge cards to maintain control over their outright price exposure. Because of the difference in tonnage between futures contracts and physical contracts, there is an inherent exposure that must be managed to reduce price risk as much as possible.

Companies also face exposure to spread risk, as discussed at length in Chapters 6 and 7. Failure to manage spread exposure correctly can lead to heavy losses. Typically, the way a company would manage this spread exposure is to maintain a **spread card**. Outright price hedge cards only include physical contracts that have had their price fixed and therefore have a corresponding futures position. Spread cards, on the other hand, include all known physical positions regardless of whether they have been priced yet or not.

A spread card comprises the following:

- Physical purchases that have been contracted but have not yet been priced,
- Physical sales that have been contracted but have not yet been priced, and
- Existing net futures positions for each monthly prompt date, for both current and future months.

By combining all their physical positions, both priced (their net futures position) and unpriced, companies will be able to view their spread exposure in every month in which they have a position. This exposure will tell them whether they can expect to be net short or long futures and in what months, hence whether they have a borrowing requirement or a lending requirement. These positions and the resulting carry trades that companies make will have a P&L impact based on the forward curve each day. Companies use their spread cards to inform both their physical trading and carry trading decisions.

Table 32 below is an example of a simple spread card a company might use to manage their spread exposure.

Table 32

LME Aluminum Spread Card December 31	Jan	Feb	March	April	May	Total
Physical Purchases						
P-XXXX	200	200	200	200	200	1,000
P-XXXX	500	500	500	500	500	2,500
P-XXXX	100	100	100	100	100	500
Subtotal	800	800	800	800	800	4,000
Physical Sales						
S-XXXX	-100	-100	-100	-100	-100	-500
S-XXXX	-200	-200	-200	-200	-200	-1,000
Subtotal	-300	-300	-300	-300	-300	-1,500
Futures	-500	0	0	0	0	0
Net	**-1,000**	**-500**	**-500**	**-500**	**-500**	**-3,000**

As you can see from the table, as of December 31, the company holds a net futures position of short 500mt in January. This would suggest it is holding 500mt of priced stock going into the end of the year. It has a total of 800mt physical purchases and 300mt physical sales pricing in each month between January and May. Based on its existing physical purchases and sales, it is getting shorter futures at a rate of 500mt per month, during this time. If the company's physical trading position doesn't change between December 31 and January 31, it will have to borrow 1,000mt or 40 lots of aluminum out of January. In this example, let's say the company borrowed those 40 lots from January to February. On January 31, its new spread card would look as it does in Table 33.

Table 33

LME Aluminum Spread Card January 31	Feb	March	April	May	Total
Physical Purchases					
P-XXXX	200	200	200	200	800
P-XXXX	500	500	500	500	2,000
P-XXXX	100	100	100	100	400
Subtotal	800	800	800	800	3,200
Physical Sales					
S-XXXX	-100	-100	-100	-100	-400
S-XXXX	-200	-200	-200	-200	-800
Subtotal	-300	-300	-300	-300	-1,200
Futures	-1,000	0	0	0	0
Net	**-1,500**	**-500**	**-500**	**-500**	**-3,000**

To add another layer of detail to a spread card, you could create a cumulative position line. This would tell you what your position would look like each month if no other changes were made. Using this same example, Table 34 shows how a company could look at its exposure and know it would be short 2,500mt or 100 lots in April. Here we have used a very small trading position that is only getting shorter by 500mt per month, so it would be relatively simple to do that calculation in your head without needing the additional cumulative row. However, most trading companies have tens, if not hundreds of positions that comprise their spread cards, so having the cumulative position row allows them to make decisions much more efficiently.

Table 34

LME Aluminum Spread Card January 31	Feb	March	April	May	Total
Physical Purchases					
P-XXXX	200	200	200	200	800
P-XXXX	500	500	500	500	2,000
P-XXXX	100	100	100	100	400
Subtotal	800	800	800	800	3,200
Physical Sales					
S-XXXX	-100	-100	-100	-100	-400
S-XXXX	-200	-200	-200	-200	-800
Subtotal	-300	-300	-300	-300	-1,200
Futures	-1,000	0	0	0	0
Net	**-1,500**	**-500**	**-500**	**-500**	**-3,000**
Cumulative	**-1,500**	**-2,000**	**-2,500**	**-3,000**	

As we have discussed, middle office employees are typically the first ones to get new information related to physical shipments. It is vitally important to be aware that failing to keep systems up-to-date will impact your company's ability to make the most effective (and hopefully profitable) decisions when it comes to spread management.

Let's say, for example, that you are the operator in charge of the above 200mt aluminum sale in February. The counterparty has requested that the pricing be moved from February to March. After discussing the situation with your trader, this request has been approved; however, you don't update your system, so you keep that sale in February. A trader or someone on the risk team looking at the spread card would be unaware that the borrowing requirement out of February had increased by 200mt because the sale was still sitting in February. They would likely reach the end of the month, and at that point they would be forced to take action. If a backwardation had developed in between confirming the change in QP to the customer and moving that sale in the system, the company would face a loss when it borrowed through the backwardation, which could have been avoided. In fact, if there was a contango at the time of the agreement to switch the sales QP, that borrow would have actually generated a profit.

Chapter Summary

- A spread exposure differs from an outright price exposure.
- Companies use spread cards to give them visibility into their forward positions and make more educated carry and physical trading decisions.
- Spread cards combine all priced and unpriced physical contracts in both the current and forward months.
- Companies typically have tens, if not hundreds of lines that comprise their spread cards. Combining these positions into one cumulative net position simplifies the management of their expected forward positions.
- Middle office employees are usually the first ones to see changes in the pricing of forward positions. It is imperative that positions are updated as soon as information is available so that any required carry trades can be made as effectively as possible.

15. Initial and Variation Margin

For every futures contract executed, the LME and CME (and therefore your broker) require a down payment to cover a percentage of the value of the trade. This payment is known as **Initial Margin (IM)**. If a counterparty that has executed a futures hedge were to face bankruptcy, the broker they had used would close out any open positions still held by that counterparty. For example, if a counterparty had open short futures positions, the broker would close them out by buying futures positions at market and vice versa for any open long futures positions. IM is held to protect against changes in exposure between the time a counterparty's exposure is calculated and the time collateral is transferred to cover that exposure. Total IM held will fluctuate as a counterparty's net futures position increases and decreases.

The amount varies by metal but as of the time of writing, for each lot traded, the IM on the LME is as follows: aluminum alloy: $6,300; aluminum: $4,350; cobalt: $2,822; copper: $17,500; NASAAC: $4,900; nickel: $17,178; lead: $4,125; lithium hydroxide: $3,309; tin: $21,575; and zinc: $6,775.

On the CME, these values are at the time of writing as follows for each lot traded: aluminum: $3,000; cobalt: $2,800; copper: $6,100; lead: $2,100; lithium hydroxide: $2,700; molybdenum oxide: 3,300; and zinc: $3,600.

The full value of the futures trade is only paid or due at the time of settlement. Therefore, a 1,000 lot copper position on the LME at a price of $10,000/mt that has a nominal value of $250 million only requires an IM payment of $13.5 million. Coming up with $13.5 million is a lot easier than $250 million! This is known as **leverage**, when your trading position value is larger than the cash you need to execute the trade.

Once the trade has been executed and the IM is financed, trading firms face another type of margin: **Variation Margin (VM)**, a continually changing figure defined by the current market price (typically the closing price each day) vs. the executed price of your futures trade(s). For example, if you sold one lot of LME copper at $9,000/mt and the current market price for copper for the same prompt date is $10,000/mt, that futures trade would carry a negative variation margin of $1,000/mt. Given that commodity companies trade significantly more than one lot at a time, you can see how quickly margin can become an issue for companies that aren't well-financed and don't manage their positions well.

These margins are typically managed under credit lines with brokers. A broker may extend a credit line to a company for IM and VM up to which it will not have to use company cash to finance those trades. For example, if a company has a $1m IM line and a $500k VM line, it can execute futures trades that require IM up to $1m before needing to finance any hedges with cash. Those hedges can move out of the money up to $500k without the need to further cash finance those open hedges.

Brokers may charge interest on these credit lines because they are essentially loans. This is one of the costs you may not have considered when thinking about trading, because it does not usually hit any P&L that you see. When your trader says that it costs $X/mt just to trade a metal, it is behind-the-scenes costs like this that make up that value.

Once a company's VM or IM is over its credit limit, it will be required to finance that position in cash by 9 a.m. London time the following day-this is what's known as a **margin call**. In extremely volatile times, it is not unheard of to face an intra-day margin call as brokers try to reduce default risks. Companies will receive notice from their broker of the amount owed. Failure to pay promptly has catastrophic consequences for a company's credit standing and trading ability.

Trading firms are typically long physical before they are short physical, so in general they are inherently short futures, and their margin will be negatively affected by rising markets and positively impacted by falling ones. With rapidly rising prices, the pressure on trading firms can be immense as they can be margin called daily with each subsequent price increase.

Chapter Summary

- Initial margin is a down payment that is required by the exchange that protects against counterparty default risk.
- The amount of the initial margin required is set by the exchange and is subject to change depending on the volatility of each commodity.
- Trading on margin allows companies to hold much larger positions than they otherwise would be able to if they were required to finance the entire notional value of the trade; this is known as leverage.
- Variation margin is the combined running mark-to-market value of all futures trades that a company has executed.
- Executed futures are valued against the current market price of that commodity (typically the closing price each day).
- Once an initial margin, variation margin, or combined credit limit is breached, a company will face a margin call and will be required to finance any overage in cash by the following morning.
- Failure to make timely margin call payments can have catastrophic consequences for that company's ability to trade.

16. Simple Option Contracts for Hedging

So far, we have looked at hedging purely from a risk mitigation perspective. However, there are situations for certain companies in which taking a relatively small amount of risk to capture an upside reward may be worthwhile. Companies in these situations can look to the options market to provide a guarantee of a hedge position while still allowing room to take a speculative position on the outright price of a commodity to increase their profits.

There are two types of options: a **call option** and a **put option**. A call option gives the holder the right to buy futures at a predetermined price-also known as the **strike**. A put option gives the holder the right to sell futures at a predetermined strike price. Option contracts will be entered into with a specific expiration date-this is the date on which the holder of the option will either exercise the option (buy or sell the underlying futures contracts) or abandon the option and take no market action.

There is, of course, a cost you are required to pay when buying options. You pay for the right to buy or sell a commodity at a given price at some point in the future, be it days, weeks, months, or even years in some cases. This is known as the **option premium**. The exact cost of an options contract premium is composed of various factors, including the price of the underlying market compared to the strike price of the contract, volatility, and time to expiry. Countless books have already been written about calculating premiums, the Greeks, and trading options on a speculative basis-so we will not go into those details here. What we will do is look at two simple scenarios that commodity companies can consider when deciding on their hedging strategies.

If you were purely speculating on a market, you might buy a call option if you were bullish on the price of a commodity, because the call option gives you the right to buy at a given strike price. Therefore, if the price of the underlying commodity increases, you can sell at market and exercise your option to buy at the lower price, locking in a profit. The opposite is true for puts. Buying a put gives you the right to sell at a given strike price, so if the underlying commodity decreases, you can buy at market and exercise your option to sell at the higher price. When utilizing options from a hedging perspective where you will own the underlying commodity, it actually works in reverse.

Let's take a buyer of physical metal; this could be a trader, or a smelter that is buying concentrates. If they were to hedge their physical purchase contract exactly as we have discussed in prior chapters, they would look to sell futures at the same time and price they agreed on for their physical purchase. However, if they believed that the price of that commodity was going to increase and were willing to pay for the right to sell at the price of the physical contract, they could buy a put option.

The option contract essentially acts as insurance in the case that the market falls in price; the option holder has paid for the right to sell at the physical contract price. However, if the market rises, they can sell at market and capture the difference between their physical contract purchase price and the market price at which they have sold futures. They will not exercise their option contract in this scenario. They will have made an additional profit if the difference between the physical contract price and the executed futures price is larger than the premium they paid to buy the put option.

If they wanted to guarantee the same price as their physical contract, they would buy a put option with a strike price that matched their physical contract price. Let's say their physical contract priced at $2,500/mt in January; they would use that same price as the strike for their put option. If they wanted to have a two-month window for prices to develop, they would set the option expiry date for March. If the premium they paid for that option was $50/mt, then they would be profitable (vs. simply hedging the contract by selling futures) once the price was above $2,550/mt. If the price stayed below $2,500/mt, they would exercise their option and would receive a March-dated futures sale with a price of $2,500/mt.

This is the same structure a miner could use when comparing their cost of production to the current market price. As discussed in Chapter 4, a straight-forward hedge for a miner would be to sell futures at market in order to lock in a gross profit margin against its cost of production, rather than waiting to receive the market price at the time they sell the concentrates. If instead of selling futures, the company buys put options, it is paying a premium in order to see if the market will rise vs. hedging at the current market price. If the market does rise more than the cost of the option, it will make additional profit. If the market falls, the insurance of the put option guarantees a futures short at the chosen strike price.

Those selling physical metal-such as a refined metal producer, or a trader-would look to buy a call option. If they were to hedge their physical sales contract exactly as we have discussed in prior chapters, they would look to buy futures at the same time and price as they had agreed on for their physical purchase. However, if they believed the price of that commodity would decrease and were willing to pay for the right to buy at the price of the physical contract, they could buy a call option. The call option provides the same insurance as in the previous example, but it gives the holder the right to buy futures at a given strike price if the market rises. However, if the market falls, they can buy futures at market and capture the difference between their physical contract sales price and the market price at which they have bought futures. If the market does fall, they will not exercise their option. They will have made an additional profit if the difference between the physical contract price and the executed futures price is larger than the premium they paid to buy the call option.

If they wanted to guarantee the same price as their physical contract, they would buy a call option with a strike price that matched their physical contract price. Let's say their physical contract priced at $2,500/mt in January, they would use that same price as the strike for their call option. If they wanted to leave a two-month window for prices to develop, they would set the option expiry date for March. If the premium they paid for that option was $50/mt, then they would be profitable (vs. simply hedging the contract by buying futures) once the price was below $2,450/mt. If the price stayed above $2,500/mt, they would exercise their option and would receive a March-dated futures purchase with a price of $2,500/mt.

This is the same structure an end consumer could use when comparing their cost of production to the current market price. As discussed in Chapter 4, a straight-forward hedge for an end consumer would be to buy futures at market in order to lock in a gross profit margin against its cost of production, rather than waiting to receive the market price at the time of actually purchasing the raw material. If instead of buying futures, the company buys call options, it is paying a premium in order to see if the market will fall vs. hedging at the current market price. If the market does fall more than the cost of their option, it will make additional profit. If the market rises, it has the insurance of the call option to guarantee a futures long at the chosen strike price.

One important factor to take into account when venturing into the options market is that there may be an open position that needs a carry trade so it does not become a physical obligation. Let's take the physical seller that wants to buy a call to give two months to see whether the price will drop. The company may have an open short position sitting in January. By potentially waiting until March to close that position out, they will create a need to borrow futures out of January. This is not necessarily a bad thing-if the market is in contango it will profit from this carry trade, and that profit can offset some of the premium it paid for the call option. But if this is not taken into consideration, it could easily end up having to borrow through a backwardation, which could negate any profit it makes on the call option.

The opposite would be true for companies that bought a put option. In this instance, those companies may have open long futures positions that would then need to be lent forward. In our example, this would be a January long futures position being lent to March. Similar to borrowing, this could be beneficial if there is a backwardation, because that carry trade would be profitable and could offset some of the premium paid for the put option. However, if there was a contango, the cost of the lend may negate the profits they might make on exercising the put option.

Depending on a company's risk tolerance, and the premiums it is willing to pay, it could utilize options for some, all, or none of their price exposure. It is simply another form of risk mitigation they can explore.

Options do have a higher up-front cost compared to a traditional hedging program, and require more specialist knowledge than executing simple outright futures. However, with the potential for large additional profits that are not attainable from simple hedging, some companies may find options an appealing alternative form of risk management.

Chapter Summary

- For companies that are willing to pay to gain either upside or downside price exposure, simple option contracts can be an attractive alternative to outright hedging.
- A call option gives the holder the right to buy futures at a predetermined price (the strike) at a defined date in the future.
- A put option gives the holder the right to sell futures at a predetermined price (the strike) at a defined date in the future.
- The cost of buying an option is known as the premium.
- A buyer of physical commodities may buy a put option as a hedge, giving them the right to sell futures. They would exercise the option only if the price of the commodity remained below the strike price of the option.
- A seller of physical commodities may buy a call option as a hedge, giving them the right to buy futures. They would exercise the option only if the price of the commodity remained above the strike price of the option.
- You must take into account any carry trades that may be required if your option expiry month is different than that of the offsetting sales or purchase QP.

17. Price Participation

In certain concentrates trades, there is a concept called **price participation**, also referred to as **scales**. It is most common in zinc concentrates trades but is sometimes seen in lead and nickel trades. Price participation involves an agreement between a buyer and seller of concentrates (typically a trader buying directly from a miner) whereby the treatment charge given by the miner increases if the underlying price of the commodity breaches a defined level.

An example of this is a trader buying 10,000dmt of zinc concentrates from a mine when LME zinc is trading around $2,700/mt and treatment charges are $160/dmt. The contract has a May shipment and a QP of M+2. The trader may try to negotiate an agreement such that if LME prices move up through $3,000/mt, the treatment charge would get an upscale (increase) of $0.10 (10%) for every $1/mt greater than $3,000/mt. Essentially, the trader would receive an additional $0.10/dmt discount for every dollar above $3,000/mt the July average price settles at.

If successful in this negotiation, the trader could sell call options that reflect the exact additional discount they would receive from the miner using the same $3,000/mt as the strike price for the option. Because they are buying 10,000dmt and the scale here is 10%, they would sell options for 10% of the total tonnage, which in this example is 1,000mt, or 40 lots. Therefore, they would sell a call option for 40 lots of zinc for average July with a strike of $3,000/mt. Options with a strike that is linked to an average price are known as **Asian options**. If instead this contract was pricing at an unknown price instead of an average-the third Wednesday cash settlement for example-then the trader would utilize **European options**. It is vitally important that the correct number of lots are sold for the option. If the calculation is incorrect, then any loss on the option would not be perfectly offset by any increase in the treatment charge and would therefore be creating a risk on the option.

Selling a call option gives the option holder the right to buy at that $3,000/mt strike price. Let's say the July average price settled at $3,100. The holder of that call would exercise that option, and the trader would have to sell at $3,000/mt and cover at market at $3,100/mt, losing $100/mt on their 40 lot option, a total of $100,000. However, they would have gained the exact same amount from their scale with the miner. The treatment charge for their purchase would have moved from $160/dmt to $170/dmt, an increase of $10/dmt on their purchase of 10,000dmt, or a gain of $100,000.

But if they are gaining the exact same amount on their physical deal as they are losing on their call option, what's the point? When you sell an option, the buyer of the option pays you a premium for the right to buy at the agreed strike price at option expiry. Once the miner has agreed upon the scale, the option premium becomes guaranteed additional profit for the trader. If the price remains below the option strike, there is no improvement in the TC, but the option expires without being exercised so the trader has still gained the option premium. If the price settles above the strike and the option is exercised, the derivative loss is exactly offset by the physical gain from receiving a higher treatment charge, and the option premium is still retained by the trader.

Let's say in this instance, when selling a call that is $300/mt out of the money with an expiry in two months, the trader may receive a premium of $20/mt, or $20,000 total, on 40 lots. The longer the expiry, or the closer the price of the strike is to the current market price, the higher the premium the trader would receive when they sell the call option. This price participation would also be more profitable the larger the upscale to the treatment charge is. The higher the percentage, the more lots the trade would be able to sell for the call option.

For scales to be a regular part of physical deals, the physical market condition is typically soft rather than tight. In very tight supply conditions, miners are less likely to share price upside with traders because the trader has far fewer options to fulfill their physical shorts. However, if supply demand conditions are such that the concentrate supply is plentiful, miners may be more willing to offer price participation as part of their contracts to secure business with the trading community.

Chapter Summary

- Price participation can form a significant part of a trader's profit margins if successfully negotiated and correctly executed.
- Whether price participation is offered is typically a reflection of the supply and demand dynamics in the market at the time of the physical purchase.
- Call options will be sold by the trader to capture a premium.
- The number of lots sold for the options contract must reflect the exact upscale of the treatment charge for every dollar the price increases past the strike.
- Any loss faced on the options contract will be exactly offset by the gain from the increased treatment charge received.
- QPs pricing on an average price require Asian options.
- QPs pricing on an unknown price require European options.
- The larger the upscale in treatment charge, the closer the market price is to the strike, and the longer the time until expiry of the option, the larger the profit will be from price participation.

18. Shanghai Futures Exchange

Although base metals globally trade primarily on either the LME or CME exchanges, domestic metals futures trading in China primarily takes place on the **Shanghai Futures Exchange (SHFE)**. The SHFE, which formed in 1999, is an amalgamation of the Shanghai Metal Exchange, Shanghai Foodstuffs Commodity Exchange, and the Shanghai Commodity Exchange. The Shanghai Metal Exchange (SHME) was formed in May 1992 and was created for trading nonferrous metals with contracts currently for aluminum, copper, lead, nickel, steel, tin, and zinc.

Base metals on the SHFE trade in Yuan (RMB) per metric ton. The exchange is open for trading between 9:00 a.m. to 11:30 a.m. Beijing time, and then again from 1:30 p.m. to 3:00 p.m.. In 2013 a night session was added that begins at 9:00 p.m. and runs until 1 a.m. the following day Beijing time for aluminum, copper, lead, nickel, tin, and zinc. In December 2014, the night session was extended to all steel future contracts as well. The night session was added to open trading during European and American market trading hours to facilitate interaction between domestic and foreign markets. It also served to expand the depth of the futures market to serve what the SHFE describes as the "real economy."

Lot sizes vary between metals on the SHFE as follows:

- Aluminum, copper, copper bc, lead, stainless steel, and zinc: 5mt lots
- Nickel and tin:1mt
- Steel rebar, steel wire rods, and hot-rolled coil: 10mt

Futures trading on the SHFE places some restrictions on non-domestic firms that the LME and CME do not have. To trade metals futures contracts on the SHFE, a company will need to become a **qualified foreign institutional investor (QFII)**. This scheme was introduced in 2002 as part of an effort to internationalize China's domestic financial markets. International investors that meet certain qualifications can directly invest in specific financial products on Chinese exchanges but they must first apply for a QFII license at the China Securities Regulatory

Commission (CSRC). Companies wishing to invest must show that they are "reputable and financially sound" under assessment by the appointed CSRC. This can include meeting certain levels of assets, equity, or liquidity. Companies must also be free from any type of disciplinary action by any financial regulatory authority within the three-year period immediately preceding their application. Once a license is acquired, the company must set up an account with a custodian bank that is approved by the CSRC, which will open trading accounts for the investor, handle the investments, and act as a liaison between the company and the CSRC.

As part of further international outreach, the requirements for obtaining a QFII were simplified in September 2020, making it easier for foreign investors to obtain this crucial qualification. The alternative for foreign companies that wish to trade on the SHFE without obtaining their own QFII is to utilize another company's qualification and trade through them, which is known as employing an agency QFII.

The one caveat to the QFII requirement for metals in China is the "copper (BC) futures contract" that trades on the Shanghai International Energy Exchange (INE). Copper BC futures were listed on the INE on November 19, 2020. This contract is very similar to the SHFE copper futures contract, but it is fully accessible to overseas investors. Deliveries are made on a bonded basis, and although tradable internationally, the contract is still denominated in RMB. The liquidity of this contract is also much lower than the SHFE copper contract, with daily volumes at the time of writing at an average of 75kmt traded vs SHFE copper with a daily volume of 750kmt.

Much like the LME and CME, the metals futures contracts that trade on the SHFE are physically settled contracts. This means that just like on the LME and CME, futures positions on the SHFE that become prompt will become physical obligations to either deliver metal into the exchange in the form of warrants if you are short futures, or receive metal from the exchange if you are long futures. Material must conform to SHFE grade and quality specifications and be stored in SHFE-designated delivery storage facilities, which are all listed by the exchange.

All base metals on the SHFE have daily trading limits both up and down for outright price changes. For aluminum, copper, copper bc, steel rebar, and hot-rolled coil, this is 3%. Lead, nickel, tin, zinc, and stainless steel have 4% limits. Wire rod has a daily limit of 5%. These limits are subject to adjustments by the exchange, which usually come when markets are especially volatile.

Initial margins for metals on the SHFE are a minimum percentage of the contract value, which at the time of writing are as follows:

- Aluminum, copper, copper bc, lead, nickel, stainless steel, steel rebar, tin, zinc: 5%
- Hot-rolled coil: 4%
- Wire rod: 7%

However, like the daily trading limits, these margins are subject to change by the exchange in times of increased volatility.

The last trading day of each month is the 15th day of each contract month. This is postponed accordingly if it falls on a weekend or legal holiday in China and would be subject to adjustment by the exchange. The last trading day of each month is also the only prompt date for base metals futures contracts each month on the SHFE. For example, if you buy January copper futures on the SHFE, your prompt date for those contracts would be the 15th day of January. You would have up until that date to either square your futures position or roll it to a different month. After the 15th day of each month, you can no longer trade futures for that month. For example, on January 16, the nearest prompt date futures would be available to trade would be the 15th day of February. Liquidity varies by metal but typically, the market rolls to the next month over the final week prior to expiry.

If a company lets a futures position become prompt with the purpose of either delivering metal or receiving metal from the exchange, there is a designated delivery period for those futures contracts, which is the two consecutive business days following the last trading day each month, except for the copper BC contract, which has a five-day delivery period following the last trading day. Warrants will either need to be received and paid for or delivered to the appropriate warehouse in this delivery window. You cannot take delivery or deliver warrants against futures contracts on any other days of the month outside of this delivery period.

One quirk of SHFE warrants is that the delivery size is different from the lot sizes that the metals trade in. For example, aluminum futures contracts trade in 5mt lots, but the delivery size for physical warrants is 25mt. To navigate this, the SHFE requires that any front month positions be adjusted to the deliverable denominations by the close of the last working day of the month prior to the expiry date. For example, for the June contract, by May 31 at 3 p.m. Beijing time, all June positions for aluminum will need to be adjusted to multiples of 5 lot denominations. Copper, lead, and zinc all have the same structure and trade in 5mt lot sizes but have a deliverable tonnage of 25mt. For nickel the deliverable tonnage is 6mt, six times the size of a futures contract. For tin, the deliverable tonnage is 2mt, two times the size of a futures contract. All steel contracts have a 300mt deliverable tonnage, 30 times the size of the futures contract, except stainless steel, which is 60mt deliverable tonnage, 12 times the size of the futures contract.

Carry trades on the SHFE involve executing two contracts for the different months separately. This differs from carry trades on the LME or the CME, where you will be quoted a simple spread between the two months and the trade is booked with the broker as a single trade. These trades are either executed manually or via computer software known as a spreader.

Futures trading related to physical contracts on the SHFE is split into two main categories: averaging and spot. A physical contract that prices over the average will reference the Shanghai Metals Market (SMM) publication price for each metal, which is published between 10:15 a.m. to 10:30 a.m. Beijing time. These prices are a function of the 10:15 a.m. front month closing price, plus the assessed physical premium for the day. Therefore, a typical averaging contract will be the SMM whole calendar month average price of the delivery month plus or minus the premium or discount. These averaging structures are usually used for long-term contracts by upstream smelters but are also occasionally used by downstream consumers as well.

A company cannot execute average trades through brokers on the SHFE, so it must have the capability to manage the execution of these trades itself. Inevitably, this means either buying or selling the net averaging exposure each day as closely as possible to the 10:15 a.m. closing price.

Some Chinese domestic long-term contracts that price over the average will take the average of the 26th day of the M-1 until the 25th day of M. This is because the government sets a deadline for VAT receipt issuance on the 25th of each month. Companies filing for VAT refunds need to know final prices for their contracts to file accordingly.

Spot trades on the SHFE are extremely liquid for base metals because of the large number of small, medium, and large traders in the market, coupled with smelters and consumers that tend to have a significant proportion of their flow under spot terms. Liquidity for these markets is rarely an issue-if you want to buy or sell a contract in large size, it is usually a matter of price and less of feasibility.

Spot trading on the SHFE is typically based on the physical market premium, which is largely correlated to market fundamentals. There are three main markets in China: Tianjin (North), Shanghai (East), and Guangdong (South), along with smaller markets inland such as Wuxi, Chongqing, and Shandong. Each of these markets commands a different premium for each metal based on the composition of the local producers and end consumers.

A typical spot trade on the SHFE would begin with the counterparties agreeing on a physical premium, followed by the pricing method. The minimum size for spot trading on SHFE is usually 30mt, which is the approximate quantity for one flatbed truck.

Either counterparty could ask for a **pricing option** (price target/level order), but typically pricing options come from the end users. If the level order is filled, it becomes the SHFE price for the transaction, with the final price being the SHFE price plus the physical premium. For example, if Company A sells 1,000mt per month to Company B, with Company B having pricing options, Company A will usually deliver the physical cargo pro rata, i.e., at 250mt per week. However, Company B can send pricing orders to Company A basis the front month SHFE contract with a "last pricing date" which is usually linked to the front month contract expiry, beyond which position rolling costs will be negotiated or Company B will be forced to price. As long as the pricing orders are filled, Company B will be deemed to have purchased the 1,000mt cargo at the average priced level for the month plus the premium or discount. Pricings orders placed prior to physical delivery require pricing deposits (usually 10% of the cargo value).

If both parties to a trade do not have price targets and are fully hedged—for example, a purchase and sale between two traders—a crossing operation on-screen without their brokers would be required. Both parties would attempt to cross their positions with no slippage (though in reality, slippage often occurs on these crosses). Brokers in China will not help you work orders; they are simply there to offer access, facilitate fund movements, and manage physical deliveries.

Of course, a large number of the transactions on the SHFE futures market are related to speculative positions, which are executed in a similar fashion to the LME and CME, with positions either squared or rolled prior to the 15th day of each month. As of September 2018 on copper, August 2020 for aluminum and zinc, and December 2022 for steel rebar, options contracts are also available to trade on the SHFE.

The SHFE imposes position limits on futures trading to ensure one single company cannot accumulate a position that could unfairly influence the market. These limits vary depending on the metal, and on which month the positions are held in. There are also different limits for FF members (SHFE brokers) compared to non FF members such as traders, producers and consumers. Table 35 details the limits as of the time of writing set by the SHFE and can also be found on the SHFE website (shfe.com.cn/eng/services/rules/shfe/).

Table 35

	From the date of listing to the delivery month		From the date of listing to the last trading day of the second month prior to the delivery month			First month prior to the delivery month		Delivery month	
	Total open Interest in a futures contract	Percentage-based position limit (in %)	Total open interest in a futures contract	Percentage-based position limit (in %) and fixed-amount position limit (in lots)		fixed-amount position limit (in lots)		fixed-amount position limit (in lots)	
		FF Member		Non-FF Member	Client	Non-FF Member	Client	Non-FF Member	Client
copper	≥80,000	25	≥80,000	10	10	3000	3000	1000	1000
			<80,000	8000	8000				
aluminum	≥100,000	25	≥100,000	10	10	3000	3000	1000	1000
			<100,000	10000	10000				
zinc	≥60,000	25	≥60,000	10	10	2400	2400	800	800
			<60,000	6000	6000				
lead	≥50,000	25	≥50,000	10	10	1800	1800	600	600
			<50,000	5000	5000				
nickel	≥60,000	25	≥60,000	10	10	1800	1800	600	600
			<60,000	6000	6000				
tin	≥15,000	25	≥15,000	10	10	600	600	200	200
			<15,000	1500	1500				
Steel rebar	≥900,000	25	≥900,000	10	10	4500	4500	900	900
			<900,000	90000	90000				
wire rod	≥225,000	25	≥225,000	10	10	1800	1800	360	360
			<225,000	22500	22500				
hot-rolled coil	≥1,200,000	25	≥1,200,000	10	10	9000	9000	1800	1800
			<1,200,000	120000	120000				
stainless steel	≥70,000	25	≥70,000	10	10	1800	1800	360	360
			<70,000	7000	7000				

A caveat to these position limits is futures trades related to physical hedges. Companies are able to hold hedge positions beyond the SHFE position limits but they will need to prove they have the equivalent physical contracts in order to do so.

With the increase in the number of QFIIs, the market structure for SHFE metals is changing. International hedge funds, banks, and traders now have much better access to SHFE trading, and with a broader range of participants, trading strategies are becoming more complex and varied.

LME and SHFE Arbitrage

We looked at definitions and explained why arbitrage trades are required in Chapter 11, but it is worth focusing on the LME/SHFE arbitrage because there are specific factors to this calculation that are not covered in that chapter. The LME/SHFE arb is a widely traded market, and the value and direction of the arb (LME premium over SHFE or vice versa) heavily influences the direction of the material flow, either metal being imported into China or exported out of China. Because SHFE prices include a domestic VAT rate of 13%, they need to be adjusted to tax-excluded prices to normalize against LME prices.

The arb is usually defined by the specific month, such as the "September copper arb." Using September as an example, the calculation of the LME/SHFE would be as follows:

The SHFE September copper price divided by the September USD/CNH exchange rate, divided by the VAT rate (currently 13%).

SUBTRACT

LME 3M Copper price +/- the adjustment to the September date.

For example:
RMB 78,900/mt divided by 7.261 divided by 1.13 = $9,616/mt
Subtract
$9600/mt - $15/mt 3M to September date = $9585/mt
LME/SHFE Arb = $9616/mt - $9585/mt = $31/mt

After taking into account the value and direction of the LME/SHFE arbitrage, to determine if it would actually be profitable for a company to import material into China or export material out of China would depend on the physical elements of the trade: physical premiums paid for the metal, financing costs, logistics costs, import and export duties, and sales premiums in the final liquidation market. These figures will vary from company to company so there is no definitive value of the arbitrage that will guarantee metal to be imported to or exported from China.

The Shanghai bonded warehouse system plays an important role in the LME/SHFE arbitrage. Material can be shipped to China and kept in bond, while the company waits for an opportune moment to capture a positive arbitrage before importing it into China for domestic consumption. Given the speed at which bonded material can be imported into China, these arbitrage windows typically do not last very long because traders look to immediately capitalize on the opportunity. Historically, there is a larger amount of copper held in bonded warehouse than other metals, making the copper arbitrage more active than the other base metals. Material can also be shipped from domestic China to bonded warehouses while the company waits for a negative LME/SHFE arb to develop; it can then be exported from China to the rest of the world. Storing metal in the bonded warehouse system does however come with costs. The handling charges to move metal into and then out of the warehouse are between \$15-\$20/mt, with additional monthly rental charges. These costs must be taken into account when considering arbitrage opportunities.

Of course, any changes to elements of the arbitrage formula will have an impact on the profitability of the trade. For example, in April 2019, China cut the VAT rate from 16% to 13%, essentially reducing the cost to import metal into China. Any changes to the USD/CNH FX rate will also impact the arbitrage calculation; this FX risk must be considered and managed accordingly if a company is to trade the LME/SHFE arbitrage.

Like outright futures on the SHFE, there is also a large speculative trading impact on the LME/SHFE arbitrage that can drive windows open or closed, independent of the physical fundamentals of the markets. However, as was seen in 2023 and 2024, with the reduction in liquidity on the back of significantly higher US interest rates and several traders pulling out of the physical market, volatility in the arb dramatically increased. Arbitrage windows stayed open longer, and wild swings from positive to negative values became more common. These scenarios make trading the arb from a purely speculative standpoint without physical flow increasingly risky.

Chapter Summary

- The SHFE is the primary exchange for trading metal futures in China.
- It was formed in 1999 and is an amalgamation of the Shanghai Metal Exchange, Shanghai Foodstuffs Commodity Exchange, and the Shanghai Commodity Exchange.
- Futures contracts on the SHFE settle in Chinese Yuan (RMB).
- Metals are open to trade between 9:00 a.m. to 11:30 a.m. Beijing time, and then again from 1:30 p.m. to 3:00 p.m.. In 2013 a night session was added that begins at 9:00 p.m. and runs until 1 a.m. the following day Beijing time.
- Lot sizes vary between metals on the SHFE and are as follows:
    - ➔ Aluminum, copper, copper bc, lead, stainless steel, and zinc: 5mt
    - ➔ Nickel and tin:1mt
    - ➔ Steel rebar, steel wire rods, and hot-rolled coil: 10mt
- Non-domestic firms must become Qualified Foreign Institutional Investors (QFII) to trade on the SHFE.
- Copper BC futures on the Shanghai International Energy Exchange (INE) are accessible to overseas investors without QFII.
- Like the LME and CME, SHFE futures contracts are physically settled.
- Warrant delivery sizes differ from futures lot sizes, necessitating adjustments to futures positions designated for physical delivery. The SHFE requires that any front month positions be adjusted to the deliverable denominations by the close of the last working day of the month prior to the expiry date.
- There is only one prompt date each month which is the 15th day of each contract month. This is also the last trading day for each month of the month. If the 15th day of the month falls on a legal holiday, the exchange will postpone the last trading day.
- Carry trades on the SHFE involve executing two futures contracts for the different months separately and are executed manually or via a spreader.
- Futures trading for physical contracts is split between spot and averaging contracts.

- A company cannot execute average trades through brokers on the SHFE so must have the capability to manage execution itself.
- Companies filing for VAT refunds will price contracts over the 26th day of M-1 until the 25th day of M, to have a final price and file accordingly by the government cutoff.
- Pricing orders are typically utilised by end users in spot trading.
- The LME/SHFE arbitrage plays an important role in the direction of metal flows.
- The Shanghai bonded warehouse system allows for metal to be stored in-bond for either import or export, depending on the current arbitrage.
- SHFE prices include a domestic VAT rate of 13%, so they need to be adjusted to tax-excluded prices to normalize against LME prices.
- Changes to VAT rates, currency rates, and import or export tariffs have an impact on the profitability of the LME/SHFE arbitrage.

19. Quiz Time

I know what you're thinking-who doesn't love a quiz?! The below questions are not here to trick you but to let yourself check to see if you have absorbed the information contained in this book. The answers to the questions will be on the pages following the quiz. You should try to answer them for the first time without referencing the main portion of the book (or just flipping straight to the answers). After you have finished the quiz, check your answers against the ones provided. If you get a perfect score, fantastic! You should feel confident in your decision-making when it comes to hedging. You can always keep this book on your desk as a quick reference in the future. If you find yourself struggling with any of the answers or don't understand a concept after reading the answer, simply go back to the relevant chapter and reread. Most importantly, never be afraid to ask someone for help. You are much better off asking questions and taking your time to fully understand a concept so you can add real value to your team, and further your personal growth.

1) What does it mean to hedge a physical contract using futures?

2) Why would a company hedge?

3) Can all commodities be hedged using futures?

4) What is a prompt date?

5) A 1,000 mt refined copper cathode physical purchase is being priced at $8,000/mt; what action is required on the futures market to hedge this contract correctly?

6) If a company hedges their price risk on their refined metals contracts, how do they generate profits?

7) What does it mean if a company assumes a perfect hedge?

8) What lot sizes do metals trade in on the LME and the CME?

9) Define a market in contango and a market in backwardation.

10) Will lending in a contango gain or lose money?

11) What is the significance of the third Wednesday on the LME?

12) What is a QP on a physical contract?

13) What is the significance of a clear paper trail when discussing QPs with counterparties?

14) Why is it important to update contracts from provisional tonnages to their final tonnages, and provisional assays to final assays?

15) A physical aluminum sales contract is priced at $2,400/mt, and the aluminum price has dropped to $2,100/mt-should you look to overship or undership if possible?

16) What is the first thing you should do if you realize you have made a hedging error?

17) What does it mean that the LME and CME are physically backed exchanges?

18) In what scenario would a company need to execute an arb trade to buy CME copper futures and sell LME copper futures?

19) Why might a company want to sell an aluminum premium forward swap contract?

20) Your company has bought a 500 mt physical zinc contract from a supplier in Europe with the purchase priced in euros. The LME price level for this contract was $3,000/mt, the premium was $300/mt, and the euro rate fixed with the customer was 1.05. How many euros would have been bought if the contract was hedged correctly? If the company waited to buy the euros until the day of

payment and the FX rate was 1.10, what would be the resulting hedge loss?

21) An operator agrees to change a QP from April to May, but they neglect to update that information in the system. What risk have they created?

22) What is variation margin? What could cause a company to face a margin call?

23) A company is hedging a physical purchase contract and is willing to pay an option premium in order to gain upside exposure to the price. Should it buy a call or a put option?

24) A company has negotiated a 20,000DMT zinc concentrates purchase contract with a 5% upscale in TC, for every $1/mt the LME price for zinc settles above $3,000/mt for a QP of average September. Should it sell European or Asian options? How many lots should it sell?

25) How many prompt dates each month do metals futures contracts on the SHFE have?

26) What is a QFII?

27) What is the delivery window for warrants on the SHFE?

28) The September SHFE copper price is RMB 76,000/mt, the current USD/CNH FX rate is 7.265, and VAT is 13%.
The LME copper 3M price is $9,000/mt, the current 3M to September adjustment is $30/mt contango.
Calculate the current September LME/SHFE arb level.

Answers

1) To hedge a physical contract, is to take an equal and opposite position on the futures market to the direction of the physical trade.

2) A company may choose to hedge for a few reasons, but the most common is to eliminate price risk from their physical contracts. They are looking to become price-agnostic so movements in price do not impact their underlying P&L. A company might also hedge to lock in profit margins where other input costs are known.

3) No, not all commodities can be hedged using futures. There must be a futures exchange that is liquid enough (trades enough volume) to buy or sell the amount of the commodity you are physically trading. Hedging is still possible for products without a relevant futures exchange, but it often involves pricing purchases and sales back to back in order to reduce exposure to changes in the price of that commodity.

4) A prompt date is the date on which your futures contract settles. LME futures can have a prompt date any business day of the month. CME futures have one prompt date per month.

5) The hedge in this example would be selling 1,000 mt of copper futures at $8,000/mt.

6) A company that hedges their refined metals price exposure is able to generate profits by buying metal at a lower premium than they sell that metal. Provided their sale premium subtract their costs is higher than their purchase premium, they will generate gross profits.

7) A company assuming a perfect hedge means they will enter into an equal and opposite futures contract for every single physical contract they execute for the exact same tonnage. As discussed in

Chapter 5, in reality, the closest a company can get to a perfect hedge is to stay within half a lot of a net-zero ton exposure.

8) LME:
aluminum, copper, lead, zinc: 25 mt
aluminum alloy, nasaac: 20 mt
steel: 10 mt
nickel: 6 mt
tin: 5 mt
cobalt: 1 mt

CME:
aluminum, lead, zinc: 25 mt
copper: 25,000 lbs (11.34 mt)
cobalt: 2204.62 lbs (1 mt)

9) When looking at two prompt dates, the market is in contango if the prompt date furthest in the future has a higher price than the nearer prompt date, meaning the price is increasing as time extends. The opposite is true for a backwardation. In a backwardation, the nearer prompt date has a higher price than the further out prompt date, meaning the price is decreasing as time extends.

10) Lending in a contango will cost money. You are selling nearby at a lower price than you are buying further out.

11) The third Wednesday of each month on the LME is the most liquid trading day of each month. It sees by far the most volume of trades settled on that day each month. Because of this, some companies choose to manage their hedge cards on a third-Wednesday-to-third-Wednesday basis.

12) A QP is the quotational period. It defines exactly how and when a physical contract can be priced-the exchange, the prompt, the method of fixing the price, any pricing options, and who has the option of declaring when a contract prices.

13) Having a clear paper trail for all QP discussions is vitally important not only because it is industry standard, but in the event of a dispute over the QP, you need to be able to prove that you detailed exactly when the contract was going to price and confirmed once the contract had been fixed. Physical metal contracts are often agreed to with very long terms and varying QP options. While contracts are indeed necessary, QP confirmations provide additional security to your hedging actions.

14) Contracts that are not updated to final weights and remain as provisional numbers create hedge exposure. By not updating tonnages, you will not be accounting for differences between final physical contract weights and the round tonnage lot sizes you are limited to hedging in. Over time, this will add up to large exposures that can cause significant losses. Similarly, contracts that are hedged using metal content percentages from provisional assays that are not subsequently updated once final assays are received, may result in an incorrect hedge position. Even small percentage changes between provisional and final assays can cause hedging expsosures that if not corrected, can also cause significant losses.

15) You should be looking to overship. The physical contract has been priced at $2,400/mt but if you overship, you will be able to hedge the additional tonnage at $2,100/mt, a profit of $300/mt on any tons you are able to overship.

16) The first thing you should do upon discovering a hedging error is immediately raise it to your manager. The quicker a hedge error is remedied, the lower the chance of a loss being incurred.

17) A physically backed or settled exchange means that if you take a futures position to its prompt date, it will become a physical obligation for that contract. If you are long futures, you will have metal delivered to you in an exchange-approved warehouse, of an exchange-approved brand. If you are short futures, you have an obligation to deliver metal in an exchange-approved warehouse, of an exchange-approved brand.

18) If a company is sourcing copper in the US and pricing that physical purchase on the CME, they would have an open futures CME short. If they then exported that copper to Europe and priced their physical sale on the LME, they would have an open futures LME long. In order to square these positions, they would need to execute an arb trade whereby they bought CME copper and sold LME copper.

19) If a company was long physical aluminum at a fixed premium and was concerned that the premiums for aluminum may fall by the time they sold the material, they could sell a forward premium swap contract to lock in their profit margin.

20) 500 mt * (LME price of $3,000/mt + premium of $300/mt)
500 * $3,300 = $1,650,000
$1,650,000/1.05 = €1,571,428.57 should have been bought to pay the supplier for the material.
If the company waited to buy the euros and the FX rate was 1.10 at the time of purchase, the same €1,571,428.57 would cost them $1,728,571.43, therefore the loss would be $1,728,571.43 - $1,650,000 = $78,571.43

21) By not adjusting the system to reflect the new sales QP of May, the additional borrowing requirement from April to May will not be reflected in the spread card. Someone using the spread card to make trading decisions will not be operating on up to date information. Should a backwardation occur by the time the position inevitably needs to be borrowed, the company will face a loss that could have been avoided.

22) Variation Margin is a continually changing figure defined by the current market price (typically the closing price each day) vs. the executed price of your futures trade(s). A company will face a margin call should the value of its total initial margin combined with its total variation margin exceed its credit line.

23) The company should buy a put option. The put option will give them the right to sell at their chosen strike price, but if the market continues to increase, they can abandon their option and sell futures at the higher market price. It will make additional profits if the value of its executed sales hedge is higher than the price of the physical contract plus the premium paid for the put option.

24) Because the QP for the physical contract is pricing over a monthly average, the company should sell Asian options. It should sell 40 lots as the upscale is 5% on 20,000dmt.
(0.05 * 20,000 = 1,000dmt = 40 lots)

25) SHFE metals futures contracts have one prompt date per month. This is the 15th day of each month unless an official Chinese holiday falls on that day. If this occurs, the exchange will postpone the prompt date accordingly.

26) A QFII stands for a Qualified Foreign Instituional Investor and is required in order for non-domestic companies to trade certain domestic Chinese futures contracts.

27) The delivery window for warrants on the SHFE is the period in which all warrant deliveries must be made in or out of the SHFE warrant system. This window is the two business days immediately following each monthly prompt date for all metals except copper BC futures, which has a delivery window of the five business days immediately following each monthly prompt date.

28) RMB 76,000/7.265/1.13 = $9,136/mt
LME 3M $9,000/mt - $30/mt contango = $8,970/mt
Current September LME/SHFE arb = $166/mt

20. Summary

Hedging itself should never be thought of as an overly complex concept. The subjects I have detailed in this book are by no means an exhaustive list of scenarios that may arise during the course of your work. But they should give you a solid base from which to continue your learning. Part of what makes the commodities industry so interesting is that no two days are the same. There are always new challenges and questions that arise, particularly when it comes to hedging.

While there are many strategies companies can take when it comes to their hedging execution and management, provided you have a firm grasp on the fundamentals of hedging, you should be able to apply that knowledge successfully and add value to your company no matter your role. While this was a guide to base metals hedging, these techniques and much of the terminology are used across all commodities. These skills are transferable regardless of the commodity you choose to work with, or as is often the case in this industry, the commodity you are told to work with!

You should never be afraid to ask questions, to review the basics, or to take your time working out the correct answer. While the commodities industry is often extremely fast-paced and you may find yourself feeling the pressure to make a decision, you are much better off checking something twice and feeling confident your decisions are correct. Rushing into an answer will more than likely lead to an error.

Speaking of errors, remember that they will happen, but how you deal with them and what you learn from them are far more important than the errors themselves.

Regardless of your long-term ambitions, be it back office, middle office, front office, or management, having a solid base of hedging knowledge will undoubtedly serve you well in your career path.

Hopefully, you now have a foundation to build from that will allow you to embrace challenges head on so your books are always perfectly hedged.

21. Glossary of Terms

Below, you will find a list of key terms from this book and their meanings. You will also find page references where these terms are discussed in the book.

Arbitrage (arb): The simultaneous buying and selling of a commodity to exploit price differences in two different markets for that same commodity.

Asian Options: The strike price of the option is based on the average price of the commodity over a defined period.

Assays: The chemical analysis of a commodity.

Average Price: The price will be set over the average of a given number of days; this could be a full month(s) or partial month average.

Backwardation: The price is decreasing with time.

Bid: The price at which you could sell.

Borrow: Buying a nearby prompt date and selling a further out prompt date simultaneously.

Buyer's Option (QP): The buyer of a commodity has the option to declare all or parts of a QP.

Call Option: Gives the holder of the option the right to buy futures at a predetermined strike price, at a specific expiration date in the future.

Carry Trade: Also known as a spread trade, this is the collective term for borrowing and lending.

Cash: A trade that is prompt two business days after the day it is traded.

Cash Settled: Trades that become prompt without being closed out are settled in cash against an agreed-upon pricing mechanism.

Contango: The price is increasing with time.

Easing: The size of a contango is increasing, or the size of a backwardation is decreasing.

European Option: The strike price of the option is based on the price of the commodity at a specific point in time.

Exchange: An institution used for the trading of commodities, such as the London Metal Exchange (LME), the Chicago Mercantile Exchange (CME), and the Shanghai Futures Exchange (SHFE).

Final Weights: The agreed-upon exact weight of a physical commodity purchase or sale.

Fixed Price: The price of the commodity for a purchase or sale has been agreed upon, often at the time of confirming the contract.

Foreign Exchange (FX) Hedging: The buying or selling of a foreign currency to mitigate exposure to changes in foreign exchange rates.

Forward Curve: Defines the value of a commodity for future prompt dates based on a single price. How far into the future the forward curve exists will depend on the commodity being traded.

Full Finance: The cost of financing an LME/CME warrant plus the cost of LME/CME warehouse rent.

Futures Contract: An agreement to buy or sell a specified tonnage of a commodity at an agreed-upon price, at a specific date in the future.

Initial Margin: A down payment required to cover a percentage or fixed amount of the value of the futures trade.

Kerb: The last of the four daily sessions on the LME.

Lend: Selling a nearby prompt date and buying a further out prompt date simultaneously.

Leverage: Executing trades with a larger nominal value than you are required to finance at the point of execution.

Long Position: You have bought a commodity.

Lot: The defined volume a commodity trades in on an exchange. For example, one LME lot of copper is equal to 25 mt.

Lowest of the Fours: The lowest official price set by the LME during the second ring between cash bid, cash offer, 3M bid, and 3M offer.

M: The scheduled month of shipment.

M-1/M-2/M-3: A minus sign after M, signals prior; M-1 would be one month prior to the scheduled month of shipment; M-2 would be two months prior to the scheduled month of shipment, and so on.

M+1/M+2/M+3: A plus sign after M, signals after; M+1 would be one month after the scheduled month of shipment, M+2 would be two months after the scheduled month of shipment, and so on.

Market on Close: The official closing kerb price posted by the LME.

Margin Call: The value of a company's combined margin has exceeded any established credit line. This exposure is required to be financed in cash once a margin call is issued.

MOAS: Month of actual shipment.

MOAS +/-: Similar to when using M, plus and minus can also be added to MOAS to define prior or after.

Mutually Agreed: Both buyer and seller of a commodity must agree to the terms of the QP.

Offer (Ask): The price at which you can buy.

Official Cash Settlement Price: The official cash offer price set by the LME during the second ring.

Open Outcry: A method of trading whereby traders set prices and transact verbally or using hand signals on a physical trading floor.

Order Depth: The number of lots available to sell or buy at a given price.

Option Premium: The cost the holder of an option contract will pay, or the amount the seller of an option contract will receive.

Perfect Hedge: Hedging to the exact same volume as your physical trade, at the exact same price.

Physically Settled: Trades that become prompt without being closed out become an obligation to either deliver metal into an exchange-approved warehouse, or take delivery of metal from an exchange-approved warehouse.

Premium: A value over and above the exchange set price for a commodity.

Premium Hedging: Mitigating the risk of buying or selling metal at an unknown future premium.

Price-agnostic: The price movements after fixing the price of a commodity do not affect the gross profitability of that contract.

Price Participation: An agreement between a buyer and a seller of concentrates whereby the treatment charge increases if the underlying price of the commodity breaches a defined level.

Pricing Option: A target level for a futures trade on the SHFE.

Prompt Date: The date a futures contract settles.

Put Option: Gives the holder of the option the right to sell futures at a predetermined strike price, at a specific expiration date in the future.

Qualified Foreign Institutional Investor (QFII): A license required to trade futures contracts on domestic Chinese exchanges.

Quotational Period (QP): Defines the terms of how the price will be fixed for a physical contract.

Ring: The name of the trading floor at the LME and also the name given to each session of trading.

Scales: An agreement between a buyer and a seller of concentrates whereby the treatment charge increases if the underlying price of the commodity breaches a defined level.

Seller's Option (QP): The seller of a commodity has the option to declare all or parts of a QP.

Short Position: You have sold a commodity.

Sifting: Picking up a large number of warrants in the hope of obtaining specific material without needing to pay a premium and delivering back the unwanted warrants.

Spread Card: A report that details a company's current and forward positions to view their spread exposure in every month which they have a position.

Third Wednesday: The most liquid prompt date on the LME each month. Also, the prompt date you are trading if you buy or sell a month. For example, if you buy 'December', your trade will be prompt the third Wednesday of December.

Trade at Settlement (TAS): The daily settlement price posted by the CME, sometimes still referred to as MOC.

Three-Month Price (3M): The standard price (and prompt date) quoted on screen for LME trading.

Tightening: The size of a contango is decreasing, or the size of a backwardation is increasing.

Tolerance: The tonnage a final delivery can differ from the contractual tonnage, usually expressed as a percentage.

Tom: A prompt date that is one business day after the current trading day.

Treatment and Refining Charges: The amount the buyer of concentrates charges the seller of concentrates to process the material.

Unknown Price: The price of a physical contract remains to be fixed.

Variation Margin: The difference in value between the price of an executed futures trade and the current market price.

Warrant: The physical parcel of metal that backs each lot of metal traded on a physically backed exchange.

PERFECTLY HEDGED

Interested in learning more?
In-person and online training available.
Visit our website for additional information.

Join the Perfectly Hedged community!
Follow us on LinkedIn for new insights,
updates and exclusive offers.

Let's connect, I'd love to hear from you:

SAMUEL BASI
Founder & Author
Perfectly Hedged LLC

+1 203-391-8021
samuel.basi@perfectlyhedged.com
www.perfectlyhedged.com
linkedin.com/company/perfectly-hedged-llc

www.ingramcontent.com/pod-product-compliance
Lightning Source LLC
LaVergne TN
LVHW100322210926
848480LV00003B/1216

* 9 7 9 8 2 9 5 6 7 0 1 1 4 *